When music lives inside you
The shadow dims

By
Kal Burgess

DEDICATION

This book is dedicated to Leo & Mary Pressey; John Burgess; Jaymee, Des, Everley, Eden & Lennon Kitchenham; Joshua, Rachel, Jaylynn & Brooklynn Kitchenham; Kayla, Joshua, Katie, & Lukas Ashe; Paula McCann: Krychelle, Tyler, Jayson & Leland Campbell; William, Amy, Mekhi, Mya, Brittany, Braden, & Asher Burgess. Sherry Spring. Tree. Lori McKenzie, Kathy, Bev & Sophie Gurski. And to Becky, James, Frank, Jessie wherever you are. Not to mention Keaunna. And to all the generations before and after.

ACKNOWLEDGEMENT

Thank you to my husband, John Burgess, who has made it possible to dare to dream. Without his love and support I would not have ventured into completing my book. He promised from the onset of our relationship to get me past all potholes on our road of love and life. My friends, Kathy Hagman, Sherry Spring and Lori McKenzie have encouraged me to take the leap and fulfill an item on my bucket list. Without the encouragement of my family, I know I would not have been brave enough to put my words onto paper for others to read. To the universe, I have arrived.

Contents

FOREWORD

I have so many poems that I started and before I was done writing them, I found they read more like a song. So, started my love of creating my own melody and lyrics. I have also had a melody in my head and took to always keeping a tape recorder with me. You could see me travelling down the road singing my heart out. Just think of my excitement when cell phones had the accessibility to do the same. I was in heaven. Since I always carried a tape recorder with me and quite often while driving home from work, having a bath, laying in bed, I'd hear these melodies, words, and music within. Now I try and capture what I hear quickly with my phone. Technology has come a long way as I didn't even have a phone in my car and my home phone didn't even have answering capabilities, except when you picked it up.

So, I started my repertoire of songs. Most no one has ever heard. Some have been sung at my church with my oldest sister carrying the soprano and I would harmonize with her. I have most of my songs on tapes or CDs. I harmonized to almost all of them. I had a good friend, Shawn, I worked with who put some guitar music to them and we even thought of starting our own band, Winter Pressey Band. Such a cool name. I almost wished I would have one more child and call the baby Winter. It was his last name and my maiden name. Dreams are important and we almost dove into that. Life got in the way and as I was moving over three thousand miles away it would have been hard to maintain.

I had set Shawn up to play with a great guitarist, John, I had met and that way they could continue a dream with my songs even. That did not come to fruition as the guitarist ended up driving me from Ontario to British Columbia. And the friendship became more, and we are now happily married for over twenty years. I apologized profusely to Shawn, and hope he understood that I needed John more than he did.

You will notice some of the lyrics are written by TOBY and some by KAL. In my growth through life I changed. I was no longer a frightened little girl coping through TOBY, but had become the woman I should be and that is when I became KAL. TOBY protected KAL from the shadows. KAL is the real me and who I am now.

So over 50 years I have been listening to tunes circle around my head. Most are just little ditties, but a few I am very proud of. I wish I was more confident and put them out there for someone professionally to produce onto their records. I am grateful to have music part of my life and I thank God for giving me this gift. Thank you to my family, John, Jaymee, Kayla, Josh, Krychelle and my parents for listening over and over as I would create them.

Most of the following were poetry converted into lyrics and will depict a little of what has been inside my head forever. Family, friends, events, feelings, etc. that I hear happening so fast I can't understand what I am hearing all the time.

So now I start the musical selections and hope someone, someday enjoys them as much as I did get them down on paper and onto cassette tapes......and now they are also a thing of the past. Who knew?
We all have inspirations –
We must bring them alive.

Without further ado let's start on a journey, a journey of music, a journey of love, a journey of hurt, a journey of just living, a journey of coming of age.

Let me take you back to a time when you were younger. Your life was full of hope and promise. You had your whole life in front of you and then will advance to the later years, after the kids, after heartbreak, after losing loved ones. And then you might understand some of who I am and maybe I can help you think of who you are.
For ease of writing, I'm going to just put everything in alphabetically and recount what was going on my life at that time. And know that I'm still working on many poems many songs. I know they'll never get heard by many, but it soothes my soul.

Up first is '**And when I close my eyes**'. This song should be about my first husband, but it's not. It's about my very first love in high school, the boy who stole my heart and my sexual desire. And at the time I needed someone in my life; when my dad had passed away, he came back in my life like he was fate to do so. He made me realize that my marriage was not a marriage anymore. After quite awhile he said he still loved me, and I knew my marriage was over, but I wasn't sure he was the one I should be with at that time in my life.

I loved him. It was like how I loved him when I was a teenager, and I was in my 30's now. I thought I was in love with him for the right reasons. I prayed that this was fateful and that we should be together.

AND WHEN I CLOSE MY EYES

And when I close my eyes at night, it's you I dream of.
I think how lucky I am that it's me you love.
And I thank God from bringing you to me.
And I think I'm as happy as I can be.

When I think back to my life before you,
There wasn't much I really wanted to do.
So, I'm trying my best to express,
My feelings of love and tenderness.

Cause when I wake up in the morning next to you,
And I know we have a love so very true.
So, I pray to God that we will always last,
Cause I know things can happen so fast.

It's when you smile at me so tenderly, I know,
You give me all your love and care for me so,
And I give all my love back to you,
And I'll love you all the years through.

And when I close my eyes at night, it's you I dream of
I think how lucky I am that it's me you love.
And I thank God for bringing you to me.
And I think I'm as happy as I can be.

And when I close my eyes at night, it's you I dream of.

TOBY

So, the boy who had stolen my heart when I was only 14 going on 15 came back into my life like a freight train. When I was around 34 there he was. And I got to say it was nice to have someone pay attention to me. We didn't see each other; we wrote letters back and forth; and we called each other. I would get upwards of a letter a day sometimes 2. And I'm sure he got as many in return. I was giddy. I realized though before I made the decision to end my marriage to be with him that I couldn't go backwards.

That was taught to me by my current husband, John. But you know fantasy works so well when you're feeling lonely.

Don't get me wrong. My first husband was a great guy. He just was complacent. He didn't want to do more, he didn't want to be more, he didn't want to change anything. I tell people if he'd had more of a backbone, we'd still be together. Not that we would fight. But he would have dug in and excelled to do more with his life; to learn more, to see more, to do more everything.

Steve filled a void in my heart. He got me to feel again. I thank him for showing me the light. Because I'm sure it was fate that brought him back in my life. And I'm sure it was fate that made me open my eyes that our relationship was not going to be good for me. But Dang, I had fun for a year and a half dreaming seeing there was more in life. I am thankful to God for letting me feel again.

And so, **Baby Can't You See** was born

BABY CAN'T YOU SEE

Tell me what it is you want from me,
Show me how it is going to be.
Hear me when I say I love you,
Help me, teach me what to do.

> Baby can't you see
> I fell in love again with you.

Hold me keep me safe and warm.
Protect me away from all harm.
Touch me any way you can.
Love me, tell me that you're my man.

> Baby can't you see
> I fell in love again with you.

Kiss me, let your lips convey your love.
Feel me and you can feel my love.
Hug me, I need your arms around me.
See me and set my heart free.

> Baby can't you see
> I fell in love again with you.

Tell me what it is you want from me.
Show me how is it going to be.
Hear me when I say I love you.
Help me, teach me what to do.

> Baby can't you see
> I fell in love again with you.
> Baby can't you see
> I fell in love again with you.

KAL 08/04/95

I did fight for my marriage. But you can only fight so long inside alone. My first husband, Jay and I met and in November of 1978; he asked me to marry him December of 1978, and we were married in June of 1979. Everyone said we wouldn't last. We weren't given years; we were given months before we would break up. It was a hard first year we both went through a lot of growing.

It was hard to get used to having someone else in my bed and someone rolling over and touching me. It took a lot out of me, and I had told Jay some of the stuff that had happened to me as a young girl, so he kind of understood. But I think it frightened him that I needed someone to be strong so that I could be weak for awhile and since It didn't happen, I became the person in charge. And that's the way Jay liked it, but I did truly love him. My mom called it the 'poor puppy syndrome'. All three of her girls picked guys that needed help in life.

Jay liked to party. His family were Alcoholics or drug users or both. That's all he knew, yeah party. He wanted more out of life when I first met him. He didn't know how to get himself out of it. I was in competition not with other girls but with drugs and alcohol and his partying family and friends. It was hard to navigate in those waters because I didn't know families that were Alcoholics or drug addicts and how to handle them. I tried to party with him without the drugs of course. That was something I couldn't put myself in. The alcohol every night, every weekend was way too much for me. Jay did quit drugs and slow down his drinking immensely and I was proud of him for that, but I still had to fight for him. It's a fight I'd do again for him.

If I could have changed one thing for him that I never did manage, that would be to feel he was enough. I blame myself for giving up after 17 years. But this one was with Jay in mind. **Be My Eternal One**.

BE MY ETERNAL ONE

I'M JUST AN OLD-FASHIONED GIRL AT HEART,
DREAMING AND HOPING WE'LL NEVER PART,
BUT YOU'VE GOT YOUR LIFE AND I HAVE MINE,
YOU JUST WANT TO BE LOVERS' TIL THE END OF TIME.

YOUR THINK IT'S CRAZY TO SETTLE DOWN
YOU LIKE TO BE OUT ON THE TOWN.
NOW BABY, DON'T YOU KNOW I LOVE YOU SO
ALL THAT YOU'RE DOING IS GIVING ME A HEART OF WOE.

COME ONE, COME ON, BE MY ETERNAL ONE.
COME ONE, COME ON, LOVE ONLY ME UNDER THE
SUN.

I'LL DO WHATEVER YOU WANT ME TO DO.
I'LL LOVE AND EVEN CARE FOR YOU.
OH, HONEY DON'T LEAVE ME HERE LIKE THIS
TO FACE THIS WORLD ALONE WITHOUT YOUR KISS

COME ONE, COME ON, BE MY ETERNAL ONE.
COME ONE, COME ON, LOVE ONLY ME UNDER THE
SUN.

COME ONE, COME ON, BE MY ETERNAL ONE.
COME ONE, COME ON, LOVE ONLY ME UNDER THE
SUN.

TOBY

When Steve came back into my life my hunger to write again exploded. He gave my heart the jump it needed to sit down and put on paper how I was feeling again. It felt wonderful. I was elated. Then the guilt would set in because Jay was oblivious to anything and everything. I would have letters from Steve on the middle of our kitchen table and not once did he question me or not give them to me. I kind of wanted him to. I wanted to discuss what was going no. I wanted to find out what his feelings truly were did he fall out of love with me? Did I fall in love with him? All those questions because someone I once loved gave me a little attention.

So many people say oh there is no such thing as fate. Or soul mates. I've got to say I thoroughly believe in fate and in soulmates. A person is so fortunate to have found their soulmate. For me, I found three soulmates in this world. There was Steve who was my high school sweetheart and then again in my 30s. Then Jay, who is the bad boy that was different than my family. And I loved him enough to marry him, enough to fight for him. Then John. I think John was always meant to be there for me at the end of my life. John is the guy who fills the potholes, so we don't have bumps on the road. My John is my most loved soul mate.

God has favored me three times. He puts them right in front of me and says this is your job you love these people. They need you to love them. But don't get content that it's only going to happen once. But I know there is no other favors coming because I am where I am where I'm supposed to be and with whom I'm supposed to be with. He's my heart; John is.

But to keep on track here. I was meant to see Steve twice in my life. He was meant to be the one I first fell in love with and the one to tell me that God was directing me away and I was done with my marriage. I needed to change my direction. And now, **'Believe Me'** was put into song.

BELIEVE ME

A letter was all it took
And you start to cloud my thoughts.
A reply was what I got
And now I'm thinking of you lots.
Again, I write to you
Try to tell you what I feel
Aching inside while I wait
Anxious waiting for how you feel

Believe me when I say
You stir an old flame
Believe me when I write
My feelings haven't changed
Believe in what you feel
Is right for only you.
Believe in yourself always
Then tell me what to do.

Can't seem to eat or sleep
Can't concentrate on things
Could it be at all possible
Could you hear my heart sing?
Cold is how my body feels
Cause you're not in my arms
Call out my name please
Come dazzle me with your charms

Believe me when I say
You stir an old flame
Believe me when I write
My feelings haven't changed
Believe in what you feel
Is right for only you.
Believe in yourself always
Then tell me what to do.
REPEAT and FADE

KAL 04/02/89

Like my poetry some songs are just that, songs. They're not always made for or written about anyone or for anyone. This would be one example of that.

I loved sitting down and putting pen to paper or most cases on my typewriter back then. That's all I had at hand - a typewriter. When I got my first computer excitement, I can put this on computer.
Well, they're saved on a floppy disk and guess what no more floppy disk. Then I got a new computer, and they are saved onto a disk. Yep, no discs anymore. Finally, a laptop and they are saved on to a CD and now laptops don't come with a CD player. So now I save everything on to a USB. I save it on my laptop I save it on the USB, and I save it on my office web so I'm not going to lose my information again. I do have good old hard copies still.

There were a few guys that I met up with; can't say I dated them. They were nice guys and I thought yeah maybe there's half a chance here with this guy. So, I kind of took my feelings for that and put them into the next song and melded them all together. Hope you like it. **But That Was Then and This Is Now**

BUT THAT WAS THEN & THIS IS NOW!!

Do you remember when we were just seven
You told me there was no God in heaven
I stayed up all night and cried and cried
I was afraid where I'd go if I died.
Then when I had just turned ten
You told me the world was going to end.
I ran to my mom and held on tight
I must have been such a frightful sight.

That was then & this is now!
You don't know why you hurt me & you don't know how.

I remember when I reached thirteen
You told me I was the ugliest girl you'd seen
I hid away from everyone
I was afraid to go out in the sun.
But when I reached sixteen things turned around
All of these things you said were unfound.
I came alive and I found a new me
There were many things I could be.

That was then & this is now!
You don't know why you hurt me & you don't know how.

At twenty-one you came back to me
You asked for forgiveness and your wife would I be
Now was my chance to get back at you
There were many things I could say and do.
So I'll forgive you and become your wife
We'll be together and have a good life
Just push all those thoughts of revenge from your mind.
The best revenge of all would be that you're mine.

But that was then & this is now!
You'll make it up to me boy and oh-oh how!!
Mm-mmmm-mm-mm-mm-mm-mm-mm-mm-mm

TOBY

Some of my faith stayed with me throughout my life. I even was the church secretary for three years. So, every now and then I'd get the spirit I guess you'd say and create a song for Christmas or Easter or just something about faith.

I never tried hard to write a religious song; it just comes out every now and then. I do firmly believe that God is above us watching over us. He is the God almighty, the Father, the Son, the Holy Ghost. Jesus came and He died on the cross to save our souls. And it's nice to think that this is true, and I say my prayers as much as I remember to do them. I feel bad because my mother never missed an evening of writing in her diary and then saying prayers. When I was a child, I said my prayers religiously. I didn't miss a Sunday church until I was over 18 years of age. I was proud that I attended church. Many nights on Saturday I wouldn't get in until probably two, three or four in the morning and I was going to church for at 9:30 with bells on. And I would say extra prayers in church for any misgivings I got up to the night before.

Calling All Angels is a hymn in my mind.

CALLING ALL ANGELS

Chorus: Calling all angels sing a song on high
For our Lord Jesus was born on this night

Sound the trumpets today
Sing out with heavenly grace
You can see His loving glory
With me look at His face

Chorus: Calling all angels sing a song on high
For our Lord Jesus was born on this night

In a small, small stable
Mary lay the Saviour down
Look He sleeps so peaceful
Making hardly a baby sound

Chorus: Calling all angels sing a song on high
For our Lord Jesus was born on this night

All around this earthly home
Everyone would soon know His Son
God had promised to the people
A soul redeemer would soon come

Chorus: Calling all angels sing a song on high
For our Lord Jesus was born on this night

KAL 17/05/10

Steve would come in and out of my life for four years during high school. We would be dating and then I didn't hear from him for a month or so. Someone would say that they ran into him and wondered where I was, and he'd say we weren't dating anymore. So, I'd wait and sure enough he would call one night, and we would talk for hours if we could get away with it that is. Party lines you know. And I would go right back, fall in love with him all over again.

And as I prepared to marry Jay, I thought of Steve a little. This little ditty is something I thought of shortly before I got married. Don't get me wrong though I was glad to marry Jay. Like I said soul mates. He was my second soulmate.

I even got up the nerve and called Steve's home about a month before I got married. I just wanted to let him know that I wouldn't be available. There would be no late-night call and I would jumped at the chance to be back with him. I wanted to tell him Jay was a great guy, and this was my step forward in life. But I didn't get to tell him that because he wasn't home. I have no idea if he tried to call my mom and dad's house to see if I was there or if he knew I was married. And you know what the thought didn't really cross my mind for years whether he did or not.

I wonder if I'd spoke up and told him if he would have shown up at the altar and confessed his love for me and whisk me away…. he never did show up and I didn't let him read this one. **Can You Feel It – Can You See?**

CAN YOU FEEL IT – CAN YOU SEE?

There's a funny feeling deep inside of me.
Something telling me what must be.
Together we have pulled away – grown apart.
Together, maybe, right from the start.
Oh, oh – can you feel it?
Oh, no – can you see?
Good things come – good things go.
It was fun, oh we should know.
We will always be such good friends.
But now our nights together must end.
Oh, oh – can you feel it?
Oh, no – can you see?
Come tomorrow I will be married.
Over the threshold I will be carried.
But there is something I must do.
Say I will always care for you.
Oh, oh – can you feel it?
Oh, no – can you see?
Oh, oh – can you feel it?
Oh, no – can you see?

TOBY

John came into my life at the right time. I trusted God to show me around and help me make an important decision. I was headed out to British Columbia from Ontario, and I wasn't coming with John to start with. I was supposed to drive north and pick up Steve and then we would head out to British Columbia. The night before I left, I said goodbye to John as a friend and he said you want me to go with you?! And I said yes.

Once we got to Cranbrook BC, I phoned Steve to let him know I was already here and if he was still serious, he should come out. Well, we've been here for almost 30 years I have yet to see him in Cranbrook so that's how serious he was. I think I made the right decision. And there is John. My hero. He's made my life 100% better and I hope I've done the same for him. He tells me I do anyhow.

The great thing is composing a few songs here and there together. Now I wish we had done more when we first got here, and our emotions were raw. Those kinds of songs are hard to write but so fulfilling. John has composed quite a few on his own, and with his band Split/Shift. I got to say they're pretty darn good. To tap into dance music, sit back and listen and have memories, back to rock and roll.

I penned this specifically for Split/Shift. I just want them to know that I really like their music and I really respect the guys in the band. They're all great musicians and composers in their own rights and together they are phenomenal. Split/Shift I hope you like this one. **Can't Do Any Wrong!**

CAN'T DO ANY WRONG

Groovin' to the beat, finding the right tone.
Nothin' better than playing the best sound.
Can't do any wrong with a guitar in hand.
The drummer's sets on fire & the bass rocks the band.

Come on get up & dance, shake your body baby.
Lights up my life when you smile for only me,
Can't do any wrong with a guitar in hand.
The drummer's sets on fire & the bass rocks the band.

Come on pretty lady, dance the night away
I'm up here singing, pouring my heart out to say
Can't do any wrong with a guitar in hand
The drummer's sets on fire & the bass rocks the band.

You can't find a better place, you know, to be
When Split/Shift gears up & the music flows free.
Can't do any wrong with a guitar in hand.
The drummer's sets on fire & the bass rocks the band.

You know you can't find a better place to be
When Split/Shift gears up & the music flows free.
Can't do any wrong with a guitar in hand.
The drummer's sets on fire & the bass rocks the band.

KAL 04/22/09

John and I did collaborate on a few and come up with some songs. I don't know if he's put music to them yet. I had just narrated, and I found a few of his starts of songs. I maybe added a little bit to see if it would make sense and someday, he will find them where he put them with a little bit extra added on. I always wonder if he will find any of them. This is one of those – **Can't seem**

Composing relaxes my soul and as I have already laid my heart out in my poetry writings book, I'm not going to go into detail some of the pain and horror I lived in, that created this young girl to have feelings that needed to be written down. Let's leave it at that!

CAN'T SEEM

What is it I thought about?
Do you remember what it was?
Can't seem to remember last night
My eyes are blurred, my mind's lost
Was it you I talked to last night?
Or did I just imagine your voice?
Can't seem to think clearly mow.
But you said I had made my choice.
Where did I go, it's just not clear?
And when did I get back here?
Can't seem to get a grasp on it.
What did I say when I was there?
Who was it I was with if not you?
Wasn't it you that I had found?
Can't seem to feel good about it all.
All that's left is to listen to no sound!

KAL & BUB 09/05/04

It's amazing as the years go on, you realize you're in a rut. You are with the person you love and you're happy, but you have become complacent. So, every now and then just remember to kick it up a notch; let your other half know you love them and would do anything for them. You'll never change your mind. Sometimes when I write, it's not because I feel that way but it's just a reminder to myself and to anybody else that listens to it. It's a reminder that life just goes too fast and even though you may feel secure and happy and in love you must let someone else know that that's how you feel about them too.

Could You Love Me? Was supposed to get my someone's attention. But it did not as I never sent it away. I was finding being with John was healing to my soul and I wanted to see where this was all going.

COULD YOU LOVE ME?

Could you love me like you use to?
Could you hold me in your arms?
Could you keep me like you use to
Away from all harm?
Could you say that you love me
Like you use to every night?
Could you hold me against your body
Warm and tight?

Chorus: I didn't know I'd miss you
In my life this much
And I didn't know my heart
Would ever be this crushed.

Could you ever forgive me from
Not knowing wrong from right?
Could you remind me that I
Should always hold you tight?
Would you take me in your arms
And hold me against your chest?
Would you look at me and whisper
I love only you the best.

Chorus: I didn't know I'd miss you
In my life this much
And I didn't know my heart
Would ever be this crushed.

Could you love me like you use to?
Could you hold me in your arms?
Could you keep me like you use to
Away from all harm?
Could you say that you love me
Like you use to every night?
Could you hold me against your body
Warm and tight?

Chorus: I didn't know I'd miss you
In my life this much
And I didn't know my heart

Would ever be this crushed

(and fade)

TOBY 96/07/05

There came a time when I knew my first marriage was over.

It didn't happen suddenly. But we just pulled away from each other. As far as I know we were faithful up until the time we knew it was over. I know that all other people thought I had something going on with John before Jay and I discussed the end of our marriage, but it wasn't like that. And even my oldest daughter told me that she thought I was having a fling with guy I did baseball stuff with, Bob. No that never happened but he was a good listener and he and his wife Phyllis made me feel just a little bit better. But you know when you stop talking to each other and you're just going through the motions it's not doing either of you any good and not doing any good for your children.

I went as far as leaving this one out on the table one night to see if Jay would even take the time to read it and ask me any questions. I guess **Did You Know?** didn't get his attention.

So, I tried prompting Jay to want more, look at a few houses for sale. But he was very complacent didn't want change never wanted to change. My third child, my second son, Josh, is much like his dad in that aspect. Josh hates change.

DID YOU KNOW?

What was it you were saying that I didn't hear?
Did you say that you loved me and wanted me near?
Was it kisses you meant to give last night in bed?
If so, why am I crying all these tears that I shed?

Did you know that I'm feeling alone and scared?
I'd say by your lack of action you didn't care.
Did you know that I'm feeling alone and scared?
I'd say by your lack of action you didn't care.

Why is it though you touch me I can't feel a thing?
Should I tell you this and give back your wedding ring?
Did I fail to see the signs that your love had died?
Can't you just say you love me or is it a lie?

Did you know that I'm feeling alone and scared?
I'd say by your lack of action you didn't care.
Did you know that I'm feeling alone and scared?
I'd say by your lack of action you didn't care.

Tomorrow is too late to take these matters in hand.
I've found someone who loves me, and I love this man
He says all the things that you can't say to me.
With all his hug's n kisses, the way it should be.

Did you know that I'm feeling alone and scared?
I'd say by your lack of action you didn't care.
Did you know that I'm feeling alone and scared?
I'd say by your lack of action you didn't care.

Do you know that now I'm not lonely or scared?
Because with all his actions he tells me he cares.
Do you know that now I'm not lonely or scared?
Because with all his actions he tells me he cares.

KAL 02/27/96

So, there I was trying to keep my marriage together. I was frustrated I was feeling very alone. I didn't know what to do. I talked to a few people got a little bit of advice from different ones. Their advice was short coming for me; it didn't match to what I could do. I loved my family. I loved being married to Jay. At the start it was hard, then I got easy, and then it wasn't there anymore. When I discussed with Jay that I had to go I had to move somewhere, and I wanted the kids to come with me. He was very upset, and he actually said he would kill himself if I took the kids. So, we made a pact that I would go. I would get settled and then the kids could come out. They could decide whether they liked it or not it was hard on him I know it was hard on me and Steve was in the middle making me very confused. And I met John as a friend, and he was going through hell with his first wife. The back story on him - I don't know how he made it through life. I do know he said he had a spot picked out where he would run his truck off the road and kill himself, but he also didn't want to leave his kids without a father.

So, Steve was willing to take me to BC. Steve said if Jay didn't want me to be his wife that he was perfectly happy to commit to me. The funny thing is though I had this feeling I needed him in my life at that point; he helped me get through feeling lost. But I had a feeling deep down feeling that what was going to happen wasn't going to be my plan. And I really needed my plan to be in place. Move somewhere make a life get my kids and grow from there.

I always felt that I wasn't enough! I wasn't pretty enough! I wasn't smart enough! I wasn't good enough! I wasn't anything enough! From childhood on I kept making bad choices.

But I did love Steve that first love kind of love that hits you – WHAM! always stays with you. We did meet up twice before I headed out to BC and that was probably a very good thing because it helped me make up my mind. The question I always had in the back of my mind – **Do You Love Me Too?**

DO YOU LOVE ME TOO?

I want to see you, hear you, be with you.
I want to love you, hug you, care for you.
I want to miss you, kiss you, hold you tight.
Tonight, and every night.

I love you; do you love me too?
Together, there's so much we can do!

We could run up, run down, run around.
We could be really quiet, make no sound.
We could hug and kiss, do anything.
We could be all or nothing.

I love you; do you love me too?
Together, there's so much we can do!

If only you'd want me, hear me, see me.
You could love me, hug me, care for me.
If you'd miss me, kiss me, hold me tight.
Tonight, and every night.

I love you; do you love me too?
Together, there's so much we can do!

I need you, want you, can't you see,
How happy our life could be?
I'd love to make you mine.
For now, and all time.

I love you; do you love me too?
Together, there's so much we can do!

TOBY

For many years I dreamt of a different life. I lived in my own imaginary world at night when I couldn't sleep. Yes, I dreamt because I couldn't sleep.

I would reimagine if I hadn't met my husband and had married one of the guys I had grew up with and dated. Especially a couple that didn't know I existed at all. Well, they knew but they saw me a 'little Deano'. I would wonder if they would have figured out that I was alive and I could be a great team member for them.

So, this one is for all the boys that didn't marry me. And for the one I did marry that had to climb out of despair to wait for me at the front of the church. Also, for the one that I almost married twice. And especially for the one that saw me for me and filled in the potholes of life for me to safely stand by his side on a hot sunny day in the middle of a park. Here is **Do You Want Me?**

DO YOU WANT ME?

Do you want me? Do you need me? Can I always depend on you?
I need to hear you say you love me, Just the same as I do you!

I really need you! I really love you! Without you, I would die.
You are my only - my one and only, And it's for you that I would try.

If I said the words for you, Could you just nod your head?
I'll start out slowly and work up gently, I'll just pretend that you said.

I really need you! I really love you! Without you, I would die.
You are my only - my one and only   And it's for you that I would try.

Now that you've got that part over, Let's move on to something else.
When I say those words for you Could you hold me against your chest?

I really need you! I really love you! Without you, I would die.
You are my only - my one and only And it's for you that I would try.

I think now we could move slowly To the rhythm of my heart
Just hold me closer – squeeze just a little. I think that you know your
part.

I really need you! I really love you! Without you, I would die.
You are my only - my one and only And it's for you that I would try.

No more pretending, no more acting. It's up to you to follow through.
I think you've got it, you learn so quickly I wonder who was teach who?

I really need you! I really love you! Without you, I would die.
You are my only - my one and only And it's for you that I would try.

I really need you! I really love you! Without you, I would die.
You are my only - my one and only And it's for you that I would try.

TOBY

I spoke of my friend, Bob. He was a saint and was one of the reasons I became brave enough to spread my wings and arrive where I am today. Bob and his wife, Phyllis, were such a warm and giving couple. They just gelled together, and I appreciated all the time Bob put into helping me feel strong. He convinced me I could coach a team of kids in baseball. He pushed me into sitting on the baseball board in our community and in our county. When I would have doubts all I had to do was talk to him and I'd continue.

He was one of the first people I said that I was leaving and moving to the other side of the country. I told him about Steve, and he did say he hoped that this guy knew what a great woman he was getting. And when I was unsure of leaving a couple nights before, he reminded me that somewhere out there, I existed as the person he saw all the potential in.

I called after I left to let them know I was safe and that he was right. Steve wasn't the guy I should be with, and that John drove me across the country safely and soundly. I almost heard a sigh of relief. Each time I go home I think of them, but time restraints and life keep us from touching base.

I know he loved Phyllis with all his heart but kept prompting him to make sure she knew the love he had for her. She was a hard-working nurse with four busy kids. I always felt she cherished the ground he walked on yet knew he was such a flirt and joker. And I also know that she'd be with him on his dying day. Although I wished him to tell her more often how he felt. So, Bob, I really hope you let her know everyday all these years – **Don't be crazy**!

DON'T BE CRAZY

Don't be crazy, tell her that you love her.
Don't be lazy, tell her that you need her.
You'll end up losing her.
You've got to get up you nerve.

Don't be like me, tell her that you love her.
Don't be like me, tell her that you need her.
I let my love slip away.
Now I want for him everyday.

Don't be crazy, tell her that you love her.
Don't be lazy, tell that you need her.
You've got time to make amends.
If you don't, you won't be friends.

Don't be like me, tell her that you love her.
Don't be like me, tell her that you need her.
If I could live my life again.
I'd tell him I love him and ease my pain.

Don't be crazy, tell her that you love her.
Don't be lazy, tell her that you need her.
You must see how she loves you.
There's only one thing for you to do.

Don't be like me, tell her that you love her.
Don't be like me, tell her that you need her.

Don't be crazy, tell her that you love her.
Don't be lazy, tell her, tell her that you love her.

TOBY

After my own dad had passed away a good friend of his asked a favour of me. The couple had visited my parents faithfully while my dad was living his last three years. They were a bit older and other people told me the wife was a shrew that nobody liked much. I found them delightful. They asked me to write a song or poem for the husband. He had found out his life was coming to his end and wanted one of my own writings to read. It took me a few weeks. **Don't be sad – be happy** was for him.

I asked my mom if she had spoken with them lately and she said that he was in the hospital. So, I packed up my tape recorder and tape with the song on it. I had the typed-up version too for them to keep with the tape. I got to the hospital, and he had was failing fast. I played the tape and gave him the printed copy with the tape. He cried and said that my dad and he would sing it together in Heaven. We lost him a few days later. As for his wife, she died shortly after as her heart was broken. I like to think they are up in Heaven sitting around a card table and singing loudly for all the other angels to hear.

DON'T BE SAD – BE HAPPY

When my time's almost here and I feel it closing in don't cry, don't be sad, be happy.

Don't you cry, don't be sad, be happy for me.
I'm still here, I'll care for you the best I can.
Don't you cry, don't be sad, be happy for me.
I'm not gone, I'll be right here for you.

When the time has come, say goodbye in your own way don't cry, don't be sad, be happy.

Don't cry, don't be sad, be happy for me.
I'm not gone, I've just went ahead of you.
Don't you cry, don't be sad, be happy for me Carry on, do the best in life you can.

Now and then think of me with a smile upon your face don't cry, don't be sad, be happy.

Don't you cry, don't be sad, be happy for me.
It's okay, I'm watching out for you.
Don't you cry, don't be sad, be happy for me.
It's okay to enjoy what we had.

I know you'll be okay till you come and join me don't cry, don't be sad, be happy.

Don't you cry, don't be sad, be happy for me.
Wear a smile for me every day.
Don't you cry, don't be sad, be happy for me.
I need you to carry on for me.

Don't you cry, don't be sad, be happy for me.
I'll always love you and know you loved me.
Don't cry, don't be sad, be happy.

TOBY

I didn't realize how needy Steve had been until later years and I looked back on the writings I had done thinking of him.

When we were teenagers, our love came in hot and heavy. He was the first guy I had spent an evening in bed, and he was a very cautious and attentive lover. I learnt a lot from him. He taught me how to kiss properly. He taught me to relax when we were together. Honestly, we could spend a couple hours just cuddling on the couch without any sex.

I will be frank and admit some nights I wanted to move onto making love, but he was content just French kissing. I think he had a little problem as he drank quite a bit, and he smoked a ton of pot. Little Steve was not always into the evening like we were. But that was okay with me too. I felt special as he wanted to still spend the evening with me.

We were on and off all through high school. Quite often after a few weeks of no calls I would find out from one of his friends or one of mine that they had run into him with someone else and he said we weren't dating. So, I would say okay and move on with life.

When we reconnected, he acted the same sometimes and I would call him and leave a message. I would write a letter almost every day, so he knew how important he was in my life. I still have all his letters. But I did find it interesting that I had some familiar feeling of that teenage girl creep into my thoughts. I think this was an ode to Steve - **Don't cry anymore**.

DON'T CRY ANYMORE

Don't cry anymore – Don't feel so down.
Don't want for anyone – Don't be afraid.
Feel with your heart – Feel alive once more.
Feel my love shining – Feel the love we've made.

Friends are people who love you.
No matter what you are like.
Friends will always be there
When life puts up a fight.
Friends are what we are
And always we will be.
Friends for ever and ever
Friends are you and me.

Don't cry anymore – Don't feel so down.
Don't want for anyone – Don't be afraid.
Feel with your heart – Feel alive once more.
Feel my love shining – Feel the love we've made.

You are important for many reasons.
One is just because you are you.
You don't need to feel so down
For you there isn't anything I wouldn't do.
You mean a lot to not only me.
But to many others you are special.
You are you and that's just fine.
My love for you will never fail.

Don't cry anymore – Don't feel so down.
Don't want for anyone – Don't be afraid.
Feel with your heart – Feel alive once more.
Feel my love shining – Feel the love we've made.

I need you to know just what I mean.
You are so special, and you should know
I would have to search forever
To find a friend so care for so.
I think you are just afraid
That if you give me all your heart
I would refuse all that love
And wish to stay far apart.

But Don't cry anymore – Don't feel so down.
Don't want for anyone – Don't be afraid.
Feel with your heart – Feel alive once more.
Feel my love shining – Feel the love we've made.

KAL 08/20/95

Many times, I would have the pleasure of talking with another woman that had love blues. They inspired me to write something new. That is the funny thing about writing – you almost must be sad or hurting to write something decent. Happy doesn't make the juices flow.

I wrote a few of my songs thinking of that person that just laid their sorrow at my feet and I do hope I helped make them feel a little better after. A few I gave a copy to, but if they are the person, I think they were that paper ended up at the bottom of their purse and found months later all crumpled up and illegible.

Mostly women would talk to me, but a few guys would tell their story at lunchtime at work or at the bar table as I listened to John and his band play. I know at this point in my life I am more interested in hearing how others are doing than how I am doing. That I will speak about later. Let's just say as you age you have a few medical worries creep up. I am waiting right now for some tests that may or may not change my life. More later.

Don't know why sprang onto the paper.

DON'T KNOW WHY?

Don't know why you can make me cry?

Don't know how you can make me almost die?

Just know you are where I should be

And I am standing here, why can't you see?

Yes, why can't you see me alone in the night?

Crying & wondering just out of your sight.

Don't know why you always seem to deny?

Don't know how you always bring tears to my eyes.

Just know you are not here holding onto me.

And I am still standing alone, Why can't you see?

Yes, why can't you see me alone in the night?

Crying & wondering just out of your sight.

Yes, why can't you see me alone in the night.

Crying & wondering just out of your sight.

Yes, why can't you see?........

KAL 03/23/09

There I was one sunny afternoon and this little repetition kept going through my head. **Floating, floating, floating, floating**. And I thought to myself, just what am I going to do with that. If memory serves me right, I was a young teenager and so I did what I did best and got out my notebook and wrote that down. Next, I put a melody to it and before long I had a song written down. One of my first songs.

Now tell me who wouldn't want to be floating up high and watch life from a bird's eye view. I have a recurring dream where I am above and watching my life in a different perspective. Usually, I have this dream when I'm pondering on something important. It helps me try and make an educated decision. I'll admit sometimes it helps and sometimes I don't recognize the warning flags and take the wrong road. Human error and human heart always get in the way of life.

FLOATING LOVE

Floating, floating, floating, floating, floating, floating

Floating above the sky so blue,
Is the feeling I hold of you.
You never really said you cared
But I could feel the love you dared.

Floating, floating, floating, floating, floating, floating

Someday soon we both will be
Floating up high in this sky so free.
Cherish this thought forever more
And again, our love will soar.

Floating, floating, floating, floating, floating, floating

Cradle me in your arms so tight
Truly love me with all your might
I love you it's plain to see
I'm in you and you're in me.

Floating, floating, floating, floating, floating, floating

Always you'll see is our love
Floating up high like a dove.
Think of me always in your dreams
Our love is floating, that's how it seems.

Floating, floating, floating, floating, floating, floating
Floating, floating, floating, floating, floating, floating

TOBY

My children, Jaymee, Kayla, Joshua and Krychelle were my focus for many years. I still worry about them and pray that they make good choices. These kids could make me so angry one moment and so proud and happy the next. Jaymee was my first and I apologize for being so hard on him. He taught me how to me a Mom and I hope he knows how much I love him. Kayla was opinionated and strong with a child innocence that made me smile. She pushed the buttons but could always hug her way out of being in trouble. Joshua was special. We weren't expecting to have more than two, but there he was. His heart is worn on his sleeve. Krychelle wasn't planned and she was. We talked about the possibility and one month after I started a new job and we had moved in with my parents we found out we would be having one more. Our family was complete.

These kids were my world. Their dad was great with them as babies and young children. He had a little difficulty as they moved up the grades in school, but he is a great father to them in adulthood. There have been bumps for sure, but my love will never wane. As of this writing I have one of my children that refuses to allow me into their life and in doing so I have lost connection with three of my grandchildren. It is nothing I can do or say to change the course they have chosen, but my doors and windows will always be open for them. The candle is on in the window to light their way back. All I can say is the 'C' word has harmed the intelligence with which they justify their actions. They throw the other 'C' word around to evaluate their chose. So, its not Cancer it was Covid that harmed our relationship. And they chose Consequences as they are reasoning. Covid protocol that made no sense and is proving to be dangerous was our reasoning not to inject unneeded unknown vaccine into our bodies.

We now are seeing proof that we did the right thing in taking the necessary precautions naturally to fend off the virus. Tears are falling from my eyes as I think that this vicious attack on all humankind caused one of my own children to become so viciously hateful to anyone that made their own choice to wait for results. Sorry I get emotional thinking about all this. Onward to '**For You Are My Little Ones**' and how my kids stay in my heart.

FOR YOU ARE MY LITTLE ONES

For you are my little ones
My pride and my joys.
For you are my little ones
My girls and my boys.
For you I'd do anything
Anything at all.
For you I'd come
Whenever you call.

I still remember
When you were all small,
My how you've grown
You're all so tall.
My arms are now empty
Empty you see.
You all mean so much
So much to me.

I know I must let go
But it's hard to do.
Because every breath
I breathe for you,
Wherever you travel
Anywhere you go.
Always remember
I love you so.

For you are my little ones
My pride and my joys.
For you are my little ones
My girls and my boys.
For you I'd do anything
Anything at all.
For you I'd come
Whenever you call.

TOBY

The first few months maybe a year I wrote quite a bit. John had given me something I had never had. He made me feel adequate. He gave me myself back. He told me daily how much he had fallen in love with me. I felt wonderful. I missed my children though, and he would hold me tight at night as my silent tears fell onto the pillow. It was such a loving awakening, yet I wasn't complete without my children. John was a trouper. He never made me feel I had made a mistake. Instead, he would encourage me to blossom and remind me I would see my children again. He was feeling the same I am sure as his three children were back in Ontario also.

I could write how I felt about him better than I could say it. I wasn't a brave lover. I was timid. He made love to me like no other man had ever done. I mean Jay was wonderful. Steve taught me basics. John told me I still had love to grow. I will never stop having the love for Jay and Steve. John though, I will forever know he loves me and that I love him with all my heart. It is funny how much love a person can have within themselves and still have room for more.

So **'Forever In Love With You'** is probably one of the first songs I wrote with John in mind.

FOREVER IN LOVE WITH YOU

My love is your love, and my heart is yours too.
I'll always love you; there's nothing I'd rather do.

Cause my love is your love and my heart belongs to you.
I'll love you deeply; forever in love with you.

My heart is yours until the end of time.
You can love me; be tender, good, and kind.

Cause my love is your love and my heart belongs to you.
I'll love you deeply; forever in love with you.

I'll always love you and for you I'll always care.
My heart is your heart and my love I'll share.

Cause my love is your love and my heart belongs to you.
I'll love you deeply; forever in love with you.

I'll always love you; you know that's true.
We'll be together our whole life through.

Cause my love is your love and my heart belongs to you.
I'll love you deeply; forever in love with you.

KAL 96/05/26

Every Christmas I love listening to all the hymns in church. My favourite hymns are from Christmas and Easter. The church is alive, and the parishioners are in the holiday spirit. People you haven't seen in church come back to worship the birth of Jesus and the death of Jesus bringing His resurrection.

I promised my mom that I would write a few hymns so **'Gather Round'** was one of my first. I was going to talk to my sister about including it in the next Christmas pageant, but our church was closing, and I didn't feel brave enough to put it out there at our next church.

GATHER ROUND

Gather round, gather round.
Listen to the merry sound.
Can you hear it? Can you feel it?
Gather round.

It's the time of year, you know
When love's so easy to show.
And if you really care
There's lots of love to share.

Gather round, gather round.
Listen to the merry sound.
Can you see it? Can you sense it?
Gather round.

I know that you want to come.
So let your heart be one.
With all the love around here.
At this wondrous time of year.

Gather round, gather round.
Listen to the merry sound.
Can you hear it? Can you feel it?
Gather round.

So now we all stand strong,
Together we'll sing along.
To celebrate his birth,
He's made our lives well worth.

Gather round, gather round.
Listen to the merry sound.
Can you see it? Can you sense it?
Gather round.

TOBY

One of the women I worked with in Ontario was reluctant to start dating again. My niece had found a very nice young man that she thought would mesh with her. We joked around about her taking the next step. I wrote a song for her but before I did that, I had this one running around in my head. Her ex was not a very nice man and ran around on her. I dedicate this one to Bonnie and the removal of her ex from her life so she could move on to the next chapter.

'Hey Mr. Sandman' was just how I imagine she felt because she had a hard time closing the door to the father of her son. Thankfully she kicked him to the curb and took the leap forward in life.

HEY MR. SANDMAN

Hey Mr. Sandman! Did you see where my love went?
Hey Mr. Sandman! He was home when I fell to sleep.
Hey Mr. Sandman! He should be home but he's not.
Hey Mr. Sandman! He should be home counting sheep.

I'm so afraid, I'm so alone.
Could you tell me what I'm to do?
He should be here right now – holding me
And counting sheep with you.

Hey Mr. Sandman! Did you see where my love went?
Hey Mr. Sandman! He was home when I fell to sleep.
Hey Mr. Sandman! He should be home but he's not.
Hey Mr. Sandman! He should be home counting sheep.

Each night I crawl in bed to go to sleep
And in my dreams, he loves me so.
But then I awake and suddenly realize
He's not here and I know not where he goes.

Hey Mr. Sandman! Did you see where my love went?
Hey Mr. Sandman! He was home when I fell to sleep.
Hey Mr. Sandman! He should be home but he's not.
Hey Mr. Sandman! He should be home counting sheep.

I cry and I try to make him understand
That I really love him so.
But try as I might and cry all night
He still gets up and he goes.

Hey Mr. Sandman! Did you see where my love went?
Hey Mr. Sandman! He was home when I fell to sleep.
Hey Mr. Sandman! He should be home but he's not.
Hey Mr. Sandman! He should be home counting sheep.
He should be home counting sheep.

TOBY

Before Jay and I were married we had a small spat. Well two weeks before the wedding to be exact. He wasn't sure he could give up the partying. His friends had spent the night before telling him to forget about the wedding and me and party with them instead.

I calmly told him as we walked down the railroad tracks in St. Thomas that he could make that decision. If he felt that drinking, doing drugs and partying your life away was what he wanted then I wouldn't stand in his way. I offered an out for him and let him know if I walked away that day, I wasn't turning back. Weddings can be unplanned. Dresses can be sold. Hearts can heal. It was his decision, but he had to know that if he wanted to get married, I was not going to be okay with drugs and drinking all the time. I am not a shrew or a puritan, but a party now and then is okay. A little drinking and friends can be a great time. I held the morals of no drugs though. He had his wild time and if we were going to settle down, make a life and have a family we had to start with our wedding. I told him that he could think about it and let me know, but not to wait too long so my parents and I could start calling family, the minister, the church, the hall, and caterers, if need be.

As I prepared to leave, he ran after me and pleaded to not let him fall back into his old ways. He didn't want to party all his life, he loved me, and he would do anything to do better in life. So, the wedding happened, and I must say I was so proud of him and the fact that he didn't drink much or do any drugs that night. We started our life together June 15, 1979.

HAND IN HAND

Hand in hand while we stroll.
Arm in arm while we walk.
Step for step I`ll stay with you.
We`re bound together like a rock.

We`ll be together thick and thin.
We`re travelling the long road of life.
Nothing will ever break us apart.
After all we`re man and wife.

Hand in hand while we stroll.
Arm in arm while we walk.
Step for step I`ll stay with you.
We`re bound together like a rock.

As the years will come and go
We`ll march through the toughest times.
For I love you and you love me
I`m all yours and you`re all mine.

Hand in hand while we stroll.
Arm in arm while we walk.
Step for step I`ll stay with you.
We`re bound together like a rock.

Hand in hand while we stroll.
Arm in arm while we walk.
Step for step I`ll stay with you.
We`re bound together like a rock.

TOBY

When I started the attempt to write a book with my poems, I reminisced how Steve had talked me into realization of my marriage to Jay was on paper mostly. And I could still feel how I felt when John gave me his advice before we even became more than friends. He told me I couldn't go backwards in life. I must move forward. And then over time he showed me how much he loved me. So, I wrote this next song with those memories in my mind.

I guess the title could be **'He Don't Love You'.** And they both were right as Jay didn't love me like Steve did. John loved me like no other and more than both Jay and Steve together.

HE DON'T LOVE YOU'

He don't love you, like I love you,
I can see it in his eyes
He don't smile, he don't caress you
I can see right through his lies
If you'd love me like you use to
I'd be the happiest man alive
But you'd have to see him like I see him
And then you'd realize

I didn't know I'd miss you so much
And I didn't know I'd long for your loving touch

He don't love you, like I love you,
I can see it in his eyes
Cause he doesn't hold you and kiss you
And gaze deep in your eyes.
If I came back, and I told you
You could see it in my eyes
That I love you, I'd kiss you
And then I'd realize

I didn't know I'd miss you so much
And I didn't know I'd long for your loving touch

Would you love, maybe forgive me
Could I see it in your eyes
Could we start over, like we once were
And see how time flies

It's time to let go, let him go
I'm right here down on my knees
I'll protect you, stand up for you
And now we can realize

I didn't know I'd miss you so much
And I didn't know I'd long for your loving touch.
And you didn't know you'd miss me so much
And you didn't know you'd long for my loving touch.
And we didn't know we miss us so much
And we didn't know we'd long for each other's touch.

'Here's My Heart' was a cry to Steve to not hurt me like he used to when we were teenagers. As afraid of that happening, I wanted to see if we were meant to be together. I believed we should be. I thought he was going to save me from myself.

I was floundering. I didn't feel loved anymore. I couldn't see where Jay and I were heading other than separate. Steve helped me get through to my heart again. I must believe that God sent him to get me to the next level in my life. Do I think we would still be together if I had gone north instead of west the day I headed for British Columbia? I have a sinking feeling that I never would have made British Columbia, I would have lost my family, and I would be all alone now. That repeats itself in my mind.

HERE`S MY HEART

Here`s my heart – please don`t break it.
Here`s my arms – to hold you tight.
Here`s my kiss – please don`t refuse it.
Here`s my love – I`m yours tonight.

Why can`t we be together
Forever and ever?
Why can`t we love each other
From now till the end of time?
Why do we need each other
Forever and ever?
And why can`t we be together
From now till the end of time?

Here`s my heart – please don`t break it.
Here`s my arms – to hold you tight.
Here`s my kiss – please don`t refuse it.
Here`s my love – I`m yours tonight.

Do you want to love me?
Forever and ever?
Do you know I love you?
From now till the end of time?
Do you want to have me?
Forever and ever?
And do you know I want you
From now till the end of time?

Here`s my heart – please don`t break it.
Here`s my arms – to hold you tight.
Here`s my kiss – please don`t refuse it.
Here`s my love – I`m yours tonight.

TOBY 95/10/06

As I sit and write this, I realize that Steve caused more angst in my life than any other man. I sing the songs to myself and look at the words and know who it is about and why I wrote it.

Don't assume that Jay had left our marriage and had a lady on the side. At least I never thought about that much. He did leave our marriage but not to be unfaithful. He just stopped caring. We didn't touch each other much. I would stay up for him to come home and he'd grunt, maybe say a few sentences and I would head up to bed while he showered and stayed up. I asked him why he didn't fight for our marriage when I was preparing to leave. He didn't really have an answer. When I said you never touch me anymore and he said because every time he touched me, he wanted to have sex. Not make love – have sex. He said he couldn't hug me and stop at that. Now I am not sure if that is a good thing or a bad thing. But I had asked him to come with me. We could all move. He refused because he was afraid of the unknown. He didn't love me enough to even say maybe that would work. I was willing to drop how I was feeling and work on our marriage, but it had to be a clean cut from where we were. We had to leave and find ourselves together. He couldn't so that was that.

'**Hey Did You Hear The Latest**?' was a mixture of me telling Steve and John what was happening in my marriage except there wasn't another woman – or maybe there was?!

I do know I found a bag of women's underwear in our closet, and they weren't mine. And they were not from the same woman unless she gained and lost weight. So, there is that? I had even asked my niece if they were hers as she stayed in that same bedroom for a bit before we had moved back to the farmhouse. They were not hers!

HEY! DID YOU HEAR THE LATEST?

Hey! Did you hear the latest? Hey! Did you hear the latest?
He`s in love with her now.
He`s gone to live with her now.
I`m left here on my own.
Where are you now I`m alone?

Hey! Did you hear the latest? Hey! Did you hear the latest?
He loves only her.
He wants to be with her.
We can be more than friends
We can be in love again.

Hey! Did you hear the latest? Hey! Did you hear the latest?
He says he`s not coming home
He left me on my own.
I`m left here on my own.
Where are you now I`m alone?

Hey! Did you hear the latest? Hey! Did you hear the latest?
Hey! Did you hear the latest? Hey!

TOBY

When Steve came back into my life, I had all kinds of emotions inside my heart and soul. I did love my husband. I did not want to leave my marriage; or I thought I did not. Or did I?

I was trying to decide what would be best for my children first when a woman I knew told me flat out that I could not do what was best for my children if I was not present and healthy in my soul. I asked God to show me a sign. I wrote down how I felt and what I was asking God in the form of a song. This is the concept of **"I Can't Believe".**

So, I was debating with myself and took a long look in the mirror. I had decided that I needed to try harder to make my marriage work. Then the sign came. I received a letter from Steve asking if I still loved him and where in my marriage was I. Now, I had to really assess my life. I remember my oldest daughter and I having a conversation about her dad as we drove into Tillsonburg. As I parked the car she got out, looked across the hood and bluntly said, "Mom, if you are not happy and dad is not paying attention to you then you should just split up before you hate each other." A second sign is how I looked at that.

I CAN`T BELIEVE

God, this is so hard to do – I love him, but still love you.
My world is tearing me apart. Do I stay here or begin a new start?

I can`t believe that I don`t know. Who it is that makes my heart
beat so?

Why does life seem so unfair? Why do I for both of you so deeply care?
I`ve never quite before realized that the previous years may be only lies.

I can`t believe that I don`t know. Who it is that makes my heart
beat so?

My head says to stick around, forget this new old love found.
My heart says go for it – you have to, you love him, so you know what to
do.

I can`t believe that I don`t know. Who it is that makes my heart
beat so?

I know he loves me with all his heart. But you`ve came back – upset my
apple cart.
I feel a bond so tight to only you. Chances like these are only very few.

I can`t believe that I don`t know. Who it is that makes my heart
beat so?
I can`t believe that I don`t know. Who it is that makes my heart
beat so?

TOBY 95/04/29

Jay and I worked full-time on opposite shifts on purpose so that childcare would be at a minimum. I worked days Monday to Friday, and he worked afternoons Monday to Friday. I left in the morning around 7am and he would get the kids up and ready. He left for his work around 2pm and I would get home shortly after 5pm. He returned around 11:30pm. This worked well in the sense that the kids didn't have both of us away at the same time.

On the weekends Jay would get up with the kids on Saturday morning and I got up on Sundays. That worked mostly because the kids went to church and Sunday school with my mom and me. Corinth Church was home to us. I went there with my parents, well mostly my mom. And my children were all baptized there.

Jay liked to work out, jog and ride bike. We lived in the country. He hated the gravel roads and the highways so he would drive into Tillsonburg and jog or bike there. I did always wonder if there may be someone else, he jogged with or biked with but never asked. He was very quiet and didn't like crowds much. I come from a big, crowded family. That was a bone of contention with him.

There was a point where I thought he was a little too close to a distant family member, yes female. I shook my head though and thought 'Nah'.

He never wanted to go to watch the kids play baseball or stuff like that. I would beg him to come but he hardly ever did. So **"I Don't Know"** was me questioning his actions.

I DON'T KNOW

I don't know what you need
Anymore from me
I don't know what you want anymore
When you walk out the door

I don't know what you do
When I'm not with you.
I don't know what I'm suppose to think
When you give her that wink?

It seems to me that you're gone
More than you're here.
It seems to be evident
That you no longer care.

I don't know what to say
When we wake up each day
I don't know how to say I love you
When my heart is so blue.

I don't know what I'll do
If you've found someone new.
I don't know how to say I don't care
When life's no longer fair.

It seems to me that you're gone
More than you're here.
It seems to be evident
That you no longer care.

It seems to me that you're gone
More than you're here.
It seems to be evident
That you no longer care.

TOBY 95/01/14

"I-I-I Don't Know Why" was more of my questioning myself and the relationship I was having with Steve. We only wrote each other and talked on the phone as he lived in Northern Ontario, and I was safe and sound in Southern Ontario.

I was wishing life was simpler and he could just whisk me away from my doubts and fears. I could not get through to Jay. Jay was retreating further and further into his own little shell. Nothing I said could bring him out. Steve was luring me from also retreating into a sombre life. He was right. Jay and I needed to do something to stay together or something to move forward separately.

I-I-I DON'T KNOW WHY

I-I-I don't know why, why, why
And I-I-I don't know why, why, why.
I don't know why I love you
And I don't know why I care.
But, Baby I do love you
And now you're here.

I-I-I don't know why, why, why
And I-I-I don't know why, why, why
I love you and you're here
And now I can say.
You are the only one
That I love everyday

You-you-you love me, me, me
And you-you-you set me free, ee, ee
And now that you
Are mine.
Things are going
To be fine.

You-you-you are the one for me.
And you-you-you make me see, ee, ee
That life is wonderful
And life is grand.
I'll be your woman
If you'll be my man.

Now-now-now is the time, time, time
And now I'll lay it on the line.
For you are the one
Who takes me there.
And you are the one
Whose life I'll share.

We-we-we must go now, ow, ow
And we-we-we- sure know how, ow, ow
We'll be together
We'll love each other
And we'll be happy

Cause we're together.

KAL 10/28/95

I have to say this next song is one of my favourite ditties. It was a light fun tune and the twists inside of it was fun to let loose. I wrote it before I was even married. I had a crush on someone that was involved already with a girl I knew. He had suggested that they were no longer dating, and we went out with my cousin and his girlfriend. It was a great evening.

The next few days I found out that his girlfriend still considered them dating and the next time the opportunity came up to go out with him, I did. I told him that while he was involved with someone, or I was dating someone we couldn't go out again.

We did go out a few times after that when we weren't seeing anyone, but he was reluctant to really date on a permanent basis so that never came to be.

"I Know That You Know" was just how he made me feel especially when I would be dating someone, and he came around.

I KNOW THAT YOU KNOW

I Know That You Know That I'm In Love With You
I Know That You Know That I Really Do
I Know That You Can't Ever Be With Me
I Know That You Really Want To Love Me

You Know That I Know What's Bothering You
You Know That I Know It's Bothering Me Too
You Know That I Would Come When You Call
You Know That I'd Give You My All

They Know That We Are Trying To Stay Apart
They Know That We Have Intertwined Hearts
They Know That We Love Each Other Deeply.
They Know That We Would Like To Be Free

We Know That They Can't Help What's Happening Now
We Know That They Just Don't Know How
We Know That They Would Feel So Down
We Know That They Need Us Around

So, We Know That They Know That You Love Me
And They Know That We Know That It Just Can't Be
Because You Know That I Know We Could Never Hurt Them
So, I Know That You Know That Our Love Will Never Win

I Know That You Know That They Know That We Know

TOBY

When Jay and I were planning to be married and there were doubts on either of our minds I penned this song to express to him how exactly I felt about life.

"I Need Someone" was how I felt at that point in time. His background family was so different from mine. I waited and gave him the option out. In his heart he wanted out, but not from me, with me from his family.

I felt we would make it and be fine. And we did for the first 10 years or so. Life got busy, we got busy, kids got busy, marriage got distant.

I NEED SOMEONE

Does It Matter That Our Life Seems Hopeless?
Do You Care If We Win Or Not?
I Can Handle This Arrangement If You Can
I Hope You Feel The Same

I Need Someone To Love Me Like You
I Need Someone Who Will Always Be True.
Please Understand That I'll Want You No Matter
And I'll Always Try To Be True.

And If Everything Goes Downhill
I'll Be Right Here By Your Side
You Can Count On Me Forever
Cause My Love Is The Kind That Lasts.

I Need Someone To Love Me Like You
I Need Someone Who Will Always Be True.
Please Understand That I'll Want You No Matter
And I'll Always Try To Be True.

I Need Someone To Love Me Like You
I Need Someone Who Will Always Be True.
Please Understand That I'll Want You No Matter
And I'll Always Try To Be True.

TOBY

In 1992, my dad passed away. He lived three years with brain tumours. He was a fighter. I missed him so much, but I was taught to continue. Life will keep going and when loved ones pass away you cope. You live. You go on.

My children were lucky enough to know him. My youngest, Krychelle, doesn't remember him as well but she was almost three when he left for Heaven.

I had to release my thoughts and **"I remember things"** was for my children so they could know their grampa Pressey through my eyes. It also gave me comfort to know he was in Heaven, and I established a reason I felt God called him home early.

I REMEMBER LITTLE THINGS

I Remember Little Things That Daddy Use To Say
I Remember Little Things Till God Called Daddy Away
I Remember Little Things That Daddy Use To Do
I Remember Little Things To Tell To You

Daddy Always Made Me Smile When I Was A Child
He Always Seemed To Calm Me Even When I Was Wild
My Daddy Could See When I Was Really Sad
And I Know He Loved Me Even When I Made Him Mad.

I Remember Little Things That Daddy Use To Say
I Remember Little Things Till God Called Daddy Away
I Remember Little Things That Daddy Use To Do
I Remember Little Things To Tell To You

Although We Never Had Much Money To Our Name
Daddy Kept Us Happy, Content Just The Same
And When Times Seemed To Be At Their Worst
Daddy's Warmth And Love Put His Family First.

I Remember Little Things That Daddy Use To Say
I Remember Little Things till God Called Daddy Away
I Remember Little Things That Daddy Use To Do
I Remember Little Things To Tell To You

A Little Joke, A Friendly Smile, A Great Big Bear Hug
A Strong Shoulder And Open Arms Of Love
These Are Some Of The Things I Keep Deep Inside
For In My Heart They Keep My Daddy So Alive

I Remember Little Things That Daddy Use To Say
I Remember Little Things till God Called Daddy Away
I Remember Little Things That Daddy Use To Do
I Remember Little Things To Tell To You

With The Wink Of An Eye, He Could Get Us To Smile
And The Way He Came In A Room Was His Very Own Style
I Know Now Why God Needed My Daddy So Soon
To Help Him Smile And Laugh When He Is Blue.

I Remember Little Things That Daddy Use To Say
I Remember Little Things Till God Called Daddy Away
I Remember Little Things That Daddy Use To Do
I Remember Little Things To Tell To You

I Remember Little Things That Daddy Use To Say
I Remember Little Things Till God Called Daddy Away
I Remember Little Things That Daddy Use To Do
I Remember Little Things To Tell To You

TOBY

As I faced the fact that my marriage was almost over, I wrote more songs. I was in pain inside, and I didn't know what would become of my family or me.

I worried a lot. I lost a lot of weight. I have a photo of myself when I arrived in Cranbrook BC. I look at it and realize that woman wasn't me. I was under 110 lbs. and that was not a good weight for me. My pants were under a size 8.

I was wondering how that happened. And I sat myself down and realized that I had been wasting away. My love was gone. My faith was shaky, and I wondered if life would ever be the same.

I wanted Jay to get out of his head and become the husband I needed. I wrote **'I Thought It'd Be Easy'**. It was a cry for him to look at our family. When he didn't seem able to do that I changed. I had decisions to make. I tried many times to get my marriage going again. I stayed up waiting for him to get home from work. I would worry during snowstorms and go out and dig out the end of the driveway at midnight so Jay would at least make it off the road. But it isn't his fault. He didn't know how to change. He had no upbringing for that.

I THOUGHT IT'D BE EASY

I thought it'd be easy, but it's not.
I thought I was crazy, but I'm not.
All I wanted to do was love you.

Weren't we in love? –
I thought you cared.
But I can see now
My love wasn't shared.

I thought you loved me, but you don't
I thought we mattered, but we don't
It's easier to cry, then to try

I don't know how –
And I don't know where,
All I know is love
Isn't fair

Maybe tomorrow would be good?
We could try over, if we could?
Please give me a chance to prove my love.

I need you everyday –
I want you in every way.
There's so much more
I could say.

I thought it'd be easy, but it's not.
I thought I was crazy, but I'm not.
All I wanted to do was love you.

Weren't we in love? –
I thought you cared.
But I can see now
My love wasn't shared.

I thought you loved me, but you don't
I thought we mattered, but we don't –

TOBY

'I'll stand right beside You' was an ode to John. We were here in Cranbrook BC. We were finding each other. We were supporting and caring for each other. He had been a mess before he offered to drive me out from Ontario to BC, but he needed to heal also. We had no idea where all this would take us.

His ex-wife was a real treat. She had torn his heart out of his chest and stomped on it so many times, he was almost suicidal. He had to get away and driving me away was as much a cure for his broken heart as it was for me. He held me as I cried missing my beautiful children and I held him when he missed his children also. It was a dependency of friendship love, and caring. We needed someone to just be there. We fell in love once we got over the hurt of a failed marriage and the absence of the ones that meant the most to both of us – our children.

I'LL STAND RIGHT BESIDE YOU

I'll stand right beside you
And catch you when you fall
Though there will be troubles
I'll see you through it all.

We can't live our lives
Thinking about the wrongs
We can only be honest
And help each other along
You are my rock to lean on
And I'll stand tall for you
I offer you my hand
And a love so strong and true.

I'll stand right beside you
And catch you when you fall
Though there will be troubles
I'll see you through it all.

I want to be there with you
Each time you need me to be
My shoulders are built for you
Lean on them you will see
We will make it together
As long as we just try
We won't give into heartache
Because now it's you and I.

I'll stand right beside you
And catch you when you fall
Though there will be troubles
I'll see you through it all.

I'll stand right beside you
And catch you when you fall
Though there will be troubles
I'll see you through it all.

TOBY 96/05/18

As I made the decision to travel to BC, I also was a little upset that Jay didn't want to come with me and that he just gave up that I was leaving.

Once I arrived in BC I wrote **'I'm leaving this Town'** was for a little healing on my end. It was a quick write and it brought to the realization that life as I knew it was now changed forever. I had made it to BC, and no one was asking to be here with me. Jay was complacent, he had manipulated the kids to now not want to come for the summer to see how they would like it.

He had threatened to end his life in even one of our children wanted to come live with me. My youngest son, Josh, heard his dad talk about all that and it frightened him. I wasn't there to soften the words and it killed me to find out that any of my children were worried about their dad's life. I tried to make sure they knew their dad would never harm himself as he loved them way too much.

I'M LEAVING THIS TOWN

I'm leaving this town, I'm not gonna to stick around
I'm out of here, cause it's been a very long year

You're not gonna like what I have to say
But I'll say it anyway
You're not gonna like what you're gonna hear
Cause it's been a very long year.

You might not like what I have to say
But I'm gonna say it anyway
You might not like what you're gonna hear
But it's been a very rough year

I'm leaving this town, I'm out, not gonna stick around,
I'm out of here, it's your life, I'm not gonna be your loving wife

You might not like what I have to say
But I'm gonna say it anyway
You might not like what you're gonna hear
But it's been a very rough long year

I'm leaving this town, I'm out, not gonna stick around,
I'm out of here, it's your life, I'm not gonna be your loving wife
I'm leaving this town, I'm out, not gonna stick around,
I'm out of here, it's your life, I'm not gonna be your loving wife

TOBY

Going along with this 'I'm feeling angry' about what was happening I wrote **'I'm not alone'** to start the healing.

I remember writing this one and acknowledging that I had to leave for my own health. It was also about the time that John had started talking to me (as my sister, Colleen and my mom had asked him to). He was supposed to change my mind about leaving Eden, Ontario.

All my life though I would tell people I am always surrounded by people and still I feel lonely. It is just my life and how I have always felt. Being the baby of seven kids you kind of blend into the décor when everyone is around.

I'M NOT ALONE

I'm not alone
I'm just lonely
I'm not happy
Why can't you see?
It's not easy to admit
It wasn't in your kiss.
I found out way too late
It wasn't you I missed.
I'm not alone
I'm just lonely

I'm not crying
Maybe it's rain
Life is crazy
Nothing is the same.
Somehow, we fell apart
We lost it somewhere
The love isn't in your eyes
But what do we care?
I'm not crying
Maybe it's rain

I'm not staying
I can't take anymore
I'm not leaving
Through the front door
One day we'll realize
What it was that went wrong
And we'll hear all about it
In a "I'm gone" song
I'm not staying
I can't take anymore.......

TOBY 96/02/27

It's so funny how I fought for my marriage and Jay. I wanted to grow old with him. I needed to feel the secure loving feeling one should feel if you are still in love though. Slowly I realized I was fighting a battle all on my own.

But at the beginning I loved Jay with all my heart, and we had a rough go, but we were together, and we were doing okay. Life was tossing and turning us over and over. Just when I would start feeling secure something stupid would happen and I'd be floundering, fighting to make sense and keep us on track.

Funny thing is that I was struggling inside to keep my head above water. I worked hard, so did Jay. Love we had for each other was not easy. People, places, things kept getting in our way. But I would work at making our love together last. I just wished he was a fighter too.

So, I wrote **'I'm not going to lose'.** It was me fighting for my love. It was me trying hard not to give in to what I knew was really happening.

I'M NOT GOING TO LOSE

Haven't I done enough for you?
What else is there for me to do?
I've tried and tried to let you go
I've done everything I know

It seems time is wearing me thin
Time seems to be going to win.
I've got to let go, oh-oh let go
But, baby, I still love you so.

No, I'm not going to lose this time
You're mine, all mine
No, I'm not going to lose time after time
You're mine, all mine, all mine

So, save your goodbyes forever
Because I'll never let go, no never
Time isn't going to win this fight
We'll start a new day after each night

No, I'm not going to lose this time
You're mine, all mine
No, I'm not going to lose time after time
You're mine, all mine, all mine

No, I'm not going to lose this time
You're mine, all mine
No, I'm not going to lose time after time
You're mine, all mine, all mine

TOBY

I admit that once fate brought Steve back into my life, I felt alive again. Here was my first love, he was hurting after losing his parents. He was tentative about writing how he felt. I was also. He wasn't attached to anyone and had no children. His road was clear. Mine, not so much. I was married. I had four wonderful and beautiful children. My dad had just passed, and I was floundering.

I tried to get Jay to talk to me about how he felt. I tried to scold myself that I needed to concentrate on everyone else. But inside I was screaming for change. I was hurting so much. That spurned me to put pen to paper again and **'I'ma Gonna Tell You One More Time'**.
I was trying to get Jay's attention. I was hoping he would sit down and listen to the words and ask questions. I, also, was hoping he wouldn't because I would have passed it off as 'nothing', just something that popped into my head one day. Well, it was something that popped into my head after I was trying to figure out how to light a fire under Jay's ass.

I'MA GONNA TELL YOU ONE MORE TIME

I'ma gonna tell you one more time that we're thru
I'ma gonna tell you just one time I don't need you
I'ma gonna tell you one more time that that's it
And I'ma gonna tell you one more time I quit.

I wish I could tell you more
But it's hard to talk thru a door
So, baby the time has come
To pack my stuff and run.

I'ma gonna tell you one more time that we're thru
I'ma gonna tell you just one time I don't need you
I'ma gonna tell you one more time that that's it
And I'ma gonna tell you one more time I quit.

I tried so hard to see
What it was you wanted me to be
But baby I need to grow
And now I need to go

I'ma gonna tell you one more time that we're thru
I'ma gonna tell you just one time I don't need you
I'ma gonna tell you one more time that that's it
And I'ma gonna tell you one more time I quit.

I know it's hard to go away
When you thought love was here to stay
And baby can't you see
You're suffocating me

I'ma gonna tell you one more time that we're thru
I'ma gonna tell you just one time I don't need you
I'ma gonna tell you one more time that that's it
And I'ma gonna tell you one more time I quit.

TOBY

'It Really Made Me Sad' was a mixture song. I had thought about my one of the guys I had kind of dated as I had been at a IRT (Independent Racing Team) dance in Orwell with my friend. It was a good time and we enjoyed dancing and drinking with a bunch of friends. I went out for a smoke with a few people and when we came back in there he was dancing with his new girlfriend.

It hurt to see him with the same girl I had seen him with a while before that. I felt more for him than he did for me, I am sure. So, the next day I wrote it thinking of how I felt about seeing him again.

The night before at the dance I had a long talk with one of his best friends, Jeff and spilled my heart without saying his name. Jeff was very nice to me and told me the guy had to be stupid not to want to date me. Yes, Jeff wanted to date me, but I had told him before that I liked him, and I was okay with hooking up once in awhile, but he was more like a brother to me, and it would be weird to date him. We could be friends with benefits before that became a normalized thing. The other guy was a good friend of my cousin's, so it didn't feel as weird.

IT REALLY MADE ME SAD

It really made me sad, maybe somewhat mad.
To see the way you held her tight, that night.
I could even feel the pain coming down like rain.
To see you love her like you loved me.

You must have seen my tears and seen all of my fears
Even though I tried to run away
I hurt so deep inside, my feelings, I couldn't hide
I know you loved her more than you loved me.

Was it something that I said or maybe something I did
That drove you to fall in love with her?
I knew it was wrong to cry, but it hurt to see love die
And to know I loved you like you were loving her.

I thought I was over you, but as soon as I seen you
I felt as though time had passed me by
I know it was so wrong to stay away so long
I still love you, but you love someone else.

It really makes me sad maybe somewhat mad
To see the way you hold her tight, tonight
I can even feel the pain coming down like rain
To know you love her like you use to love me

Ya, it really makes me sad....

TOBY

One night I was supposed to go out with Steve, but he called and said he had a lot of work to do so I called my friend, Sherry and we went to The Aylmer Hotel for a few drinks. The band wasn't too bad, and we danced some. Around 10:30pm I was thinking it would be nice to surprise Steve and stop in to say goodnight.

Boy, was I surprised to see him sitting in his living room with another girl? Oh ya, she's just a friend and only dropped in to say hello. Um, no I don't think so Steve. Try again. I was very sad, and this broke us up for a little while. Creative juices run better on sadness than on happiness.

I know I truly loved Steve from the first night we met. And if he had asked me to leave and go away with him, I would have. **'It's All I Can Do'** was my response to having my heart crushed and yet I still loved him. If he had called the next day telling me how sorry he was I would have jumped up and down to forgive him. He didn't, and he dated that girl for a short time, and I could only imagine it had been going on before that night. Honestly, she was one of the loosest girls from Aylmer. A couple weekends after that Sherry and I came up behind them on the back road and he couldn't drive fast enough to try and shake us off his tail. My dad's Oldsmobile Delta 88 had more guts in it than his old Ford truck. We stayed on his tail from Corinth to Springfield. Once we got there, I decided we would go a different way. A couple weeks after that he called me finally and asked if I wanted to come over. So, it was on again for whatever time he saw fit to grace me with his love. I know that all this heartache and falling in and out of the love so easy was my way of facing the shadow I saw on my bedroom wall. My relationships were always a way to escape from my own personal trauma.

IT'S ALL I CAN DO

It's all I can do to stay away from you
I know it's true, but what else can I do.
It's all I can do cause I still love you.
And you belong to her

I've tried so hard to let go
I've tried so hard you know.
And every time I see you
I still want to be yours

It's all I can do to stay away from you
I know it's true, but what else can I do.
It's all I can do cause I still love you.
And you belong to her

Mm, mm,mm,mm,mm.........

It's all I can do to stay away from you
I know it's true, but what else can I do.
It's all I can do cause I still love you.
And you belong to her

We never should have gave up
We were so much in love
But she came in between us
Now your love is hers

It's all I can do to stay away from you
I know it's true, but what else can I do.
It's all I can do cause I still love you.
And you belong to her
And you belong to her

TOBY

At our little village church Corinth United, we put on Christmas plays and what not. I loved singing hymns. I loved being in the plays also. I wrote **'It's Christmas'** hoping one Christmas I would be asked to do it. I am still waiting…...and I'll wait forever as it closed in the 1990's.

I still wrote this one with that dream in my thoughts. You know, shine my light, and let everyone know I was a poet and a songwriter. Each time I wrote something I felt no one would want to hear it anyways. I didn't tape myself singing my songs until I was in my 30's. I still hold back to this day. Writing this book is a healing for me. If you are reading it, then I finally got the nerve to publish it. And if you are reading it, I thank you. I just want to share a little of me with someone else.

IT'S CHRISTMAS

It's Christmas, it's Christmas – a time for love – it's Christmas.
It's Christmas, it's Christmas – a time for love – it's Christmas.

This is the time of love and cheer.
A time for friends and family is here.
You can feel a closeness all around.
Feelings of togetherness can be found.

It's Christmas, it's Christmas – a time for love – it's Christmas.
It's Christmas, it's Christmas – a time for love – it's Christmas.

And one must remember why this is so,
It all happened on a night long ago.
Into this world, Christ did come.
To right all wrong which we had done.

It's Christmas, it's Christmas – a time for love – it's Christmas.
It's Christmas, it's Christmas – a time for love – it's Christmas.

So, as we all sit down to pray,
There are so many things we should say
To ask forgiveness for things we have done
But most important, thank God for his Son.

It's Christmas, it's Christmas – a time for love – it's Christmas.
It's Christmas, it's Christmas – a time for love – it's Christmas.

TOBY

I left for BC in March of 1996. John drove me out here. It took a few years for me to write how I felt letting go of my marriage. By the time I wrote this one I was remarried to John and happy. I still had this little sadness to shake loose and of course writing about it helped.

'It's Time to Say Goodbye' was for my own healing. I had written the first few lines years before and found them scribbled down in one of my workbooks. One day when I was sitting alone, I finished it. It was therapeutic for me.

IT'S TIME TO SAY GOODBYE

Not going to make excuses, not going to start to cry.
We might as well admit its time to say goodbye

It's been a long time since we laid in each other's arms.
Glowing in the throes of love, all spent, happy & warm

Not going to make excuses, not going to start to cry,
We might as well admit its time to say goodbye.

Do you really remember when we first fell in love?
Days passed so quickly; we just couldn't get enough.

Not going to make excuses, not going to start to cry.
We might as well admit its time to say goodbye.

It's not easy trying to hold onto a love gone wrong.
But heaven knows it's been going bad so long.

Not going to make excuses, not going to start to cry.
We might as well admit its time to say goodbye.
Not going to make excuses, not going to start to cry.
We might as well admit its time to say goodbye.

KAL 03/23/09

My kids were the stars in the sky for me and I loved them so much. I know I made a lot of mistakes as they grew up, especially the oldest two. I was not a relaxed mother and felt inadequate at most times, but I was also stubborn and couldn't reach out and ask others for guidance. That was one of my biggest mistakes. As the baby of the family, I was not confident and sure of anything. I wanted to be a better mom but also was scared that I would be too lenient.

As they grew older, I wrote a few poems and songs about them. I remember one night sitting at the kitchen table singing into my machine and redoing it over and over. From my mom's side of the house my two youngest ran into the kitchen and my son, Joshua, stopped and hushed the youngest, Krychelle, and whispered to her, 'sshhh, mom's singing about us, just listen'. I felt so proud he realized it.

So, **'It's You I Love'** was one of my finest about how much I loved my children. I listen to this song at least once a day as it is on my playlist in my van.

Sad thing for me is that my oldest son, Jaymee, has cut me out of his life and I am unable to see my three beautiful granddaughters. He preplanned to not allow me to be part of their life. Why? Because I made a choice of what I put in my body and what I do not put in my body. Yep, the dreaded vaccine that was not tested thoroughly, but force upon most Canadians. I stood up and said no thank you and so he first referred that if family loved his own family they would rush out and get jabbed. And worse yet he made a reference that I was selfish for not complying. With all the adverse effects I am still not vaccinated and will remain so until I grow old and pass on when God deems it time. Meanwhile though I miss my granddaughters everyday. I love them regardless of how their father has chosen to treat his own mother and I pray he never have to feel the heartless hurt he threw upon me.

May God show him mercy as his own children grow older and have minds of their own. I had to get that off my chest. I feel like I am going to explode into tears and never stop crying.

IT'S YOU I LOVE

Wherever you may go
Whatever you may do
Always remember, I'll love you.
Whoever you become
I'll never change my mind
It's you I love.

From the first time I saw you
Cradled in my arms
I already knew I'd protect you from harm.
From the first step you took
I was always there for you
It's you I love.

To the rough years you will have
Learning about love,
I'll do my best with the help of God above.
You'll always have me
To count upon
It's you I love.

Life may seem hard
When you first leave the nest
But honey, I know you gave it your best
You're always in my heart
Go follow your dreams
Remember, it's you I love.

Wherever you may go
Whatever you may do
Always remember, I'll love you.
Whoever you become
I'll never change my mind
It's you I love.

TOBY 93/07/10

'Just a Story' took a few years to write. I started it when I was a teenager and finished it after I was married. It was about me, but it also was about how we fall in love and then out of love so easily. It brings to light how a person may feel once the love is all gone, and they have had to move on in their lives.

For many when love falls apart there is a lot of residual feelings. For me writing about it helps make more sense of the toil inside my heart. If you have never loved and lost it is hard to understand. It would be so nice if people could just fall in love together and remain so until the end of time. We have lost that loving happily ever after feeling. Well, maybe not lost it but forgot about it. I love my husband John with that happily ever after feeling. What is scary though is if I hadn't met Jay, fallen in love, married, had our wonderful children, I would never have met John. Nor would I have had a special place in my heart for Steve over the years.

JUST A STORY

This is a story, it's a sad one I must tell
But it's a story that I know so very well
She tried to make him happy, but she couldn't
She tried to make him love her, but he wouldn't

This man, her drove her wild, she was filled with desire
He never understood how much he set her on fire

I know you've heard this story many times before
So what's it going to hurt to hear it one time more
You know she tried so very hard to please him\
She should have realized her love would never win.

This man, he drove her wild, he set her heart on fire.
He would never know she was filled with a deep desire.

She tried so many times to make him look at her.
She did everything to attract him, I'm sure
But you know he was too busy to even realize
So she left him and now she's got on with her life

This man, he drove her wild, he set her heart on fire.
He would never know she was filled with a deep desire.

So now she sits alone and finds it very hard
To pick up her life and the pieces of her heart
But I know she did the right thing in the end
He was not for her to have, not now or even then

This man, he drove her wild, he set her heart on fire.
He would never know she was filled with a deep desire.

This is a story, and it's a sad one I must tell
But it's a story that I know so very well.
I'm sure by now you know why that can be
For that woman wasn't a stranger, it was me
This is a story and it's a sad one I must tell

TOBY

John is my happily ever after, but life sure brings bumps and potholes also. I know as we age, we have a wonderful and strong bond. As we come closer to the end of our mortality, I know we need more time. We need **'Just One More Minute'.**

We have laughed more and loved stronger. I can honestly say John gives me more love and is far more attentive than I am. I try to be as free and laidback as he is. I must remind myself that every moment we are together it is vital that we enjoy each other.

When John falls asleep I will sit and watch him. I am jealous that he can sleep at the drop of a hat. But when I watch him, I admire the man he is. I wish I had met him when my dad was alive. They would have gotten on great. But then again, I never would have met John if my dad had lived longer. It was because my mom went to the Plum Creek Pickin' Parlour at Roger Longs that I did meet him. If my dad had lived, I don't think mom and dad would have gone out to listen and dance there. Maybe they would have, but that is for another lifetime to find out.

JUST ONE MORE MINUTE

Just one more minute is all that she said
Just one more minute to make our love last

There was a time we'd laugh at life
Nothing else mattered we were husband & wife
Time was playing along, it was our love song

Just one more minute is all that she said
Just one more minute to make our love last

We never understood time had worn us thin.
How life is fragile, wasting it is a sin
Time was playing along, it was our love song

Just one more minute is all that she said
Just one more minute to make our love last

The end of our time is just around the bend
We've one last chance to let loose our hearts and mend
Time was playing along, it was our love song

Just one more minute is all that she said
Just one more minute to make our love last
Just one more minute is all that she said
Just one more minute to make our love last

TOBY 11/03/27

Near the end of my marriage and before I had to make the decision to move along, I wrote how I felt into a song. It is a depressing and slow song. It is almost morbid. I feel like it tells of a death. It is a death. A marriage ending.

I do wish Jay had shown more interest into what I liked doing and what the kids did. Maybe life would have taken a different turn.

'Less Said', allowed me to release some of the worry and sadness I held inside.

LESS SAID

Less said, less said, you say is best for us.
Less said, less said sometimes is too much.
Less said, less said what am I to do?
Less said, less sad and now I'm leaving you.

You never want to talk with me. I'm never on your mind.
The less I talk to you each day, Seems to suit you fine.
Each day I say less to you, Each day we drift apart,
Soon there won't be any room For words inside my heart.

Less said, less said, you say is best for us.
Less said, less said sometimes is too much.
Less said, less said what am I to do?
Less said, less sad and now I'm leaving you.

Each time I walk in the room You seem to turn off your ears.
Each time I get close to you, You shy away – Is it me you fear?
I can see a rising mountain And soon I'm not going to climb.
If you don't soon start to listen, I'm sure I'll lose my mind.

Less said, less said, you say is best for us.
Less said, less said sometimes is too much.
Less said, less said what am I to do?
Less said, less sad and now I'm leaving you.

Somehow a raging river Has come between us.
When I ask what's wrong? You say don't fuss.
My body starts to tremble In fear you know.
When I see you go away And know not where you go.

Less said, less said, you say is best for us.
Less said, less said sometimes is too much.
Less said, less said what am I to do?
Less said, less sad and now I'm leaving you.

You never smile at me All I see is a frown.
Was it something I said That brought you so down?
If soon you don't open up And tell me what is wrong
I'll just burst wide open And won't be here for long.

Less said, less said, you say is best for us.
Less said, less said sometimes is too much.
Less said, less said what am I to do?
Less said, less sad and now I'm leaving you.

TOBY 95/05/25

'Let's Say It's Over and Say Goodbye' made a statement of me letting go. I was falling into the thought that I couldn't save my marriage to Jay and that I had to make some difficult decisions.

Before I go further, I must clear up that the decisions I had to make were to keep my children with me. I was made a promise that they would be allowed to go with me. Unfortunately, some thought I was being selfish as I left. The most selfish was the breaking of a promise. I cannot be mad at why the promise was broken. But I can say it was broken because Jay was broken. He fell into a despair and made it clear to most that he would have no reason to live if the kids came with me.

He told me if they left, he would kill himself. I made a deal that they come out and see how they like it and that I would make sure they came back to see him whenever they wanted and if they didn't like it, I would get them home to Ontario.

What many didn't know is that I was dying inside for a couple years before I made the decision. My departure was to keep me alive for my kids. I was losing a lot of weight. I was falling into a depression that almost encompassed me. I dove into keeping myself so busy I wouldn't have to think. I didn't care if I ate or slept. If it wasn't for my kids, I would have just drifted away slowly until I disappeared into the fog. But for those who feel I was being selfish I understand that. Maybe I was selfish to want to live. And maybe I was selfish to want the best for my children also.

Many do not know how close I was to the edge. That is because I smile and don't share my inner most feelings with many. I continue to do that. Smile, smile, smile and no one will know how you feel inside. Smile no matter what. Smile if someone says anything asking if you are alright.

LET'S SAY IT'S OVER AND SAY GOODBYE

YOU SHOULD'VE KNOWN I WASN'T HAPPY
BY THE WAY I CRIED AT NIGHT.
YOU SHOULD'VE SEEN THAT I WAS CRYING
SAID YOU LOVED ME, HELD ME TIGHT.
YOU SHOULD'VE KISSED ME MORE OFTEN,
GAZED WITH LOVE INTO MY EYES.
BUT NOW I FOUND SOMEONE WHO LOVES ME,
LET'S SAY IT'S OVER AND SAY GOODBYE.

And I'd just like to say, that I'm leaving today.
I can't lie anymore and now I'm walking out the door.

HE CALLS ME HONEY EVERY DAY
AND HE REALLY MAKES ME SMILE
HE EVEN SHOW HOW MUCH HE LOVES ME
THOUGH HE'S FAR AWAY MANY MILES
HE TELLS ME WHAT COULD MAKE HIM HAPPY
HOW I'M A BIG PART OF HIS LIFE
AND SAYS THAT IF YOU CAN'T LOVE ME
HE'D BE THRILLED, MAKE ME HIS WIFE.

And I'd just like to say, that I'm leaving today.
I can't lie anymore and now I'm walking out the door.

I KNOW YOU'VE TRIED YOUR BEST TO LOVE ME
IT'S JUST YOU NEVER KNEW HOW.
I SHOULD'VE TOLD YOU SOONER WHAT HAPPENED
BUT I JUST COULDN'T UNTIL NOW
I CAN LOVE HIM SO VERY EASY
IT'S HARD TO EXPLAIN AND THIS IS WHY
HE'S ALWAYS BEEN INSIDE MY HEART
LET'S SAY IT'S OVER AND SAY GOODBYE

And I'd just like to say, that I'm leaving today.
I can't lie anymore and now I'm walking out the door.

MmMmMmMmMmMmMmMmMm.........
Let's just say it's over and say goodbye.

TOBY 95/11/11

I have two version of **'Lord If you are Listening'.** They both speak directly into my heart. One was missing the one person I needed the most in my life – my dad. I wish he had lived longer so I could have appreciated having him. I felt lost that he never knew why I had guarded my heart so much. Why I pulled away from family. He never got a chance to protect me because I didn't tell him when I was hurt and who hurt me.

The second version was more of an ode to God and my dad. I like both versions and I know they both need to be part of my life.

LORD IF YOU ARE LISTENING

I cried the day you went away
I dried my tears and went on
Then I had nothing more to say
So, I was gone before long
You never reached out for me
And I was lost you know
I packed my bags yet again
I was gone before the first the first snow.

Lord, if you're listening
Please make me a blue bird
So, I can fly away home
Lord is you're listening
Please make me a blue bird
So, I can fly away home
I heard from someone today
Said that God had called you home
I thought about you again
And now I feel all alone

Lord, if you're listening
Please make me a blue bird
So, I can fly away home
Lord, if you're listening
Please make me a blue bird
So, I can fly away home
I wonder if I will ever smile
I miss where I use to be
I need to see my home
Lord, can you hear me

Lord, if you're listening
Please make me a blue bird
So, I can fly away home
Lord, if you're listening
Please make me a blue bird
So, I can fly away home

KAL 02/26/15

LORD IF YOU ARE LISTENING #2

I stand before you today
I get down on my knees
When I had nothing more to say
I was gone before long
You never completely left me
And I was lost you know
I packed my bags yet again
I was gone before the first the first snow.

Lord, if you're listening
Please make me a blue bird
So, I can fly away home
Lord is you're listening
Please make me a blue bird
So, I can fly away home
I heard from someone today
Said that I should come back home
I thought about you again…….And how I feel all alone

Lord, if you're listening
Please make me a blue bird
So, I can fly away home
Lord, if you're listening
Please make me a blue bird
So, I can fly away home

I wonder if I will ever smile
I miss where I use to be
I need to see my home
Lord, can you hear me

Lord, if you're listening
Please make me a blue bird
So, I can fly away home
Lord, if you're listening
Please make me a blue bird
So, I can fly away home

KAL 03/02/15

'Loving You is Easy'.........this one was over a few years. I had the chorus written down and it took a few years for the body to come together. I'll admit at first it was started when Steve was still in the picture a little, but John had just become a friend. Once we drove out west to British Columbia, I dug it out once we had our own place and finished it off.

John was mostly my muse on this one.

Side note today is July 15ᵗʰ and we celebrate 22 years of marriage. It doesn't feel that long honestly. It feels like yesterday that we stood in front of friends and family and promised each other to be there through it all.

LOVING YOU IS EASY

Loving you is easy, Being yours is what counts
I'm yours; take me. Let our love, upon wings mount.

Believe me when I tell you how much I care
Because, darling, you matter so much to me
I could never leave you; oh, I wouldn't dare.
Being in love with you just comes naturally.

Loving you is easy, Being yours is what counts
I'm yours; take me. Let our love, upon wings mount.

We've had bad times, but think of the pleasant,
They are the special memories I hold of you,
Lying in your arms, (so warm and safe,) thinking what it means
Takes me to bright days when our love was true.

Loving you is easy, Being yours is what counts
I'm yours; take me. Let our love, upon wings mount.

I promise you one thing – I love you with all my heart.
And honey I'll never let my love fade.
Remember this and hopefully we'll never part
Just lie together on hot days under the shade.

Loving you is easy, Being yours is what counts
I'm yours; take me. Let our love, upon wings mount.

TOBY

My sister, Colleen, passed away in 2017 from a blockage in her duodenum after a successful surgery on her stage 4 pancreatic cancer. I couldn't attend her celebration of life, but my heart was there with all the family. Colleen and Elizabeth were wonderful sisters to have. Colleen was the mother hen for many. I was in the middle of a trial that would send me to 'Camp Cupcake'.

Then in 2018 my loving mom went to join her in the clouds. I couldn't attend because of constraints on my travel. And I had my two daughters that couldn't attend along with their children, so I did the next best thing and held onto my daughters while my wonderful nephew, Stephan, facetimed us the service.

My mom and Colleen were matriarchs for our families. And they could bake up a storm. So, I was able to collect my thoughts on this while doing my stint at camp. I started it for Colleen then finished it for mom. **'Mama's Going to Candy Heaven'** is for both.

MAMA'S GOING TO CANDY HEAVEN

Mama's going to Candy Heaven
At least that's what she told me today
She cried as she said she doesn't want to go
But God needs her to come right away.

He needs her to make her sweet candy
Up in Heaven for all of His people there.
And the sooner she can come the better
And she'd make lots so they can share.

Mama's going to Candy Heaven
At least that's what she told me today
She cried as she said she doesn't want to go
But God needs her to come right away.

And she promised she'd make me more candy
She'd show me how to make it just like her.
So, one day I could come to Candy Heaven
And again, we could finally be close and near.

Mama's going to Candy Heaven
At least that's what she told me today
She cried as she said she doesn't want to go
But God needs her to come right away.

Mama's going to Candy Heaven
And God needs her to come right away
Mama's gone to Candy Heaven
We buried her today....

KAL 18/04/16

'*Merry Christmas Little Ones*'. I never sang it for anyone except when my children were small. I have always wished I could have been brave enough to sing it at church one Christmas.

I am not a brave soul. I have always been shy at first. Some put it down as I was haughty and thought better of myself. Quite opposite. I felt lower than everyone around me. My family was well known in our community. My brothers all played ball and hockey. My sisters were outgoing and well liked. My parents were loved by everyone. I felt like an ugly duckling. I was sure I was an outsider.

But I dreamt of singing my songs loud and proud even if it was just a Christmas song and at our small church in the small hamlet of Corinth.

MERRY CHRISTMAS LITTLE ONE

Merry Christmas little one
Happy New Year to everyone!
This is the time we all talk about
Lift up your voices and shout.

Merry Christmas little one
Happy New Year everyone!
This is the time of the year
Friends and family come near.

Merry Christmas little one
Happy New Year to everyone!
A time for love and for joy
A time for girls and for boys.

Merry Christmas little one
Happy New Year to everyone!
This is the time we all talk about,
Lift up your voices and shout.

Merry Christmas little one
Happy New Year to everyone!
Jesus was born on Christmas day
He came to take our sins away

Merry Christmas little one
Happy New Year to everyone!
This is the time we all talk about
Lift up your voices and shout

Merry Christmas little one
Happy New Year to everyone!
This is the time we all talk about.
Lift up your voices and shout.

TOBY

While I was still in Ontario and working at Canadian Tire in Tillsonburg I had a good friend, Bonnie, that worked in the office with me. She was trying to get out of a bad situation with her narcissistic husband. Once she did, she blossomed with each day. Bonnie was hooked up with a young man that also had been looking for someone who would just love him.

We talked a lot and with much encouragement she relented and decided to give love another go. **'Mr. Sunshine'** was for Bonnie and Phil, her new chance to love.

They married and had a beautiful little girl to add to their family along with her son from that previous union. I was so happy they fell in love.

MR. SUNSHINE

Mr. Sunshine, shine down on me. I'm so glad and happy.
Mr. Sunshine, shine from above Tell the whole wide world that I'm in
love.

I'm telling you right from the start
You came along and stole my heart
Tell me now is this for real –
The kiss upon my lips; your seal.

Mr. Sunshine, shine down on me. I'm so glad and happy.
Mr. Sunshine, shine from above Tell the whole wide world that I'm in
love.

I never know how great love felt
Til the wall fell down and the ice did melt.
I know now I've a lot of love to give
And now my life I'll start to live.

Mr. Sunshine, shine down on me. I'm so glad and happy.
Mr. Sunshine, shine from above Tell the whole wide world that I'm in
love.

From this day on it'll be you and me.
We'll make it through, just wait and see.
I am your soul, you are my life
And soon we'll be husband and wife.

Mr. Sunshine, shine down on me. I'm so glad and happy.
Mr. Sunshine, shine from above Tell the whole wide world that I'm in
love.
Tell the whole wide world that I'm in love.

TOBY

I have found over the years that I love singing this one a lot. It was for my children and now includes my grandchildren.

When my kids were young, I loved singing in the car with them. I wasn't an easy mom to my kids, but I would do anything for them. When I had to leave in 1996, it tore my heart in four. A piece for each of them. I have recently discovered that one of my kids considers that move as selfish and has stated that I continue to be selfish and only think of myself. That tore my heart in two more fragments.

I did move without my children, but they were always supposed to come and try out British Columbia with me. They all did at some point and three came to stay finally. One returned to Ontario, and we talk almost more than the kids here.

I am so proud of my children and wish they could read why it was so important for me to leave Eden Ontario. I believe, for the most part, they do. The one that has frozen me out of his life doesn't get the trauma I held onto living there. I pray some day he realizes that it was my love for my children that took me away. If I had stayed, I would have disappeared from their life forever. Although, recent events may finally be what takes me away.

'My wonderful, wonderful little ones' was about the four sets of feet running around our house.

MY WONDERFUL LITTLE ONES

You are my wonderful, wonderful little ones
You are the ones who make life so much fun.
My wonderful, wonderful little ones.

I'd climb mountains to see
The shine is your eyes
I'd swim oceans to be
Alone you and I

Cause you are my wonderful, wonderful little ones
You are the ones who make life so much fun
My wonderful, wonderful little ones.

And when nothing goes right
You come to me
I hold you so tight
The way it should be.

Cause you are my wonderful, wonderful little ones
You are the ones who make life so much fun
My wonderful, wonderful little ones.

All the clouds go away
When you come to stay
And the sun seems to say
Have a happy, happy day.

Cause you are my wonderful, wonderful little ones
You are the ones who make life so much fun
My wonderful, wonderful little ones

TOBY

'No Man's Wife' was a cry for attention from my first husband when we were first married. I was losing the battle of keeping him from drinking himself to death I thought. Every visit to any of his friends or family resulted in him drinking way too much. It was a cause for worry for me. I had never lived with anyone that drank like his family. Nor had I known people that did drugs so recreationally all the time.

I was sure our marriage was doomed. I wrote this thinking that at some point soon it would be over. Although, I was determined to prove those that thought we wouldn't make it wrong.

NO MAN'S WIFE

This is the end
There's no going back.
I can't go on
I can't stay here.

I've tried so hard
To be what you want
But being what you want
Just isn't enough

Come this time tomorrow
I'll be gone from your life.
Got my life all together
I'll be no man's wife.

I always wanted
To be a good wife.
My ideas were different
Then yours from the start.

So, when I leave
Out through the door,
Let me take this –
My name – not yours!!

Come this time tomorrow
I'll be gone from your life.
Got my life all together
I'll be no man's wife.
I'll be no man's wife.

TOBY

John and I have a few collaborations. Some he was present for and some he started but didn't finish. I even saved a few of his from certain death of the round metal can – known as file thirteen to some.

'Not as Young as we used to be' is one I don't even remember working on. I hope John remembers it and the music to go with it.

It is kind of catchy and not too long to lose interest like some marriages. Not ours though. John and I are forever. Well not too much longer as we age. It is eye opening to figure out that in anywhere from 10 to 30 years you will not be walking on this earth.

NOT AS YOUNG AS WE USE TO BE

I fell in love with
A much younger you.
I still see that (wo)man
When I look at you.

Time has passed, oh so quickly.
We are not as young as we use to be.

We wake each morning
And go thru our days,
Not realizing how
Time is slipping quietly away

Time has passed, oh so quickly.
We are not as young as we use to be.

It's hard to find the time
To show our true thoughts
We should slow down
Come let's take a shot

Time has passed, oh so quickly.
We are not as young as we use to be.
We are not as young as we use to be.

KAL & BUB 03/23/09

'Oh, I Miss Her So' is a song I wrote in case John's band came up dry creatively. I am sure they never will.

Split/Shift is John's band and they have been together quite a while. John originally was in Copper Creek with some friends. It was a slow ballad to country style band. John loved playing with them, but he also was more of a rocker.

He started his own little band and slowly they have found a sound. A lot of drummers have come, gone, returned, left again. Drummers are hard to keep. But John, Cub, Mike, and Emilio have been together a long time.

John is deaf and plays by memory. It is hard for him, but I am so proud of him.

OH, I MISS HER SO

The dishes are dirty in the sink tonight
And now she's left on the 9:30 flight
It's way too quiet, there are no sounds
And now she's living in another town

I waited too long to finally see
That woman did really love me
Like a fool though I let her go
The love of my life. Oh, I miss her so.

She tried to tell me what was going wrong
I didn't listen to her so now she's gone
She'll be in someone else's arms tonight
Mine are empty, my head isn't feeling right

I waited too long to finally see
That woman did really love me
Like a fool though I let her go
The love of my life. Oh, I miss her so.

She told me more than once she was not okay
I pretended I didn't hear what she had to say
I imagine she is loving him like she loved me
I hope, he can see her and love her deservedly

I waited too long to finally see
That woman did really love me
Like a fool though I let her go
The love of my life. Oh, I miss her so.

KAL 97/02/12

The next song I think I've only sang for my mom once. I did put it on a tape for her before I moved out west. I now listen to it at least once a week as a drive. I have some of my music, some of John's, some of Colleen's and my dad. Mixed in there is Garth Brooks and some old country songs.

'Oh, mom can you see?' is for the woman that showed me how to be, well to be me. My mom was phenomenal. She just had that knowledge of who she was. Although, I do know she had wanted to be a missionary in another country before my dad came along. So, seven kids later, almost eight, she was mom to our family and to many other souls on the road of life.

After I moved away, she called every week, and I called her also. We could talk about anything and yet not talk about the stuff we didn't want to share. She knew if I sounded off and I knew if she did. We may have been 3,000 miles apart, but we still had a bond that only a mom and daughter could. As she aged, we talked about the end. She made me promise not to get all weepy and fly home if her time came up. She had said the same thing to my sister Beth when our gramps was failing.

You don't have to be present in the same room to feel the love. When mom passed, I stayed, but she was here with me. I feel her still. It is calming to know she is still present for her family. Mom, I miss you, but I know you know how much I loved you. You are in my heart as I will be with mine, especially my daughters. They say your daughters are your mothers as your granddaughters are yours. I think that is a wonderful way to think.

OH MOM, CAN YOU SEE?

Oh mom, can you see what it is that I am?
Oh mom, can you see what it is that I am?
I'll be what I'll be, I'll do what I'll do.
Oh mom, can you see I'm just like you?

You taught me how to be a good wife
Just by the way you loved my dad.
You showed me how to do the best
With anything that I had.

Oh mom, can you see what it is that I am?
Oh mom, can you see what it is that I am?
I'll be what I'll be, I'll do what I'll do.
Oh mom, can you see I'm just like you?

I try so hard to be very good.
And show my children my love.
You taught me to pray and to give thanks
And believe in our God up above.

Oh mom, can you see what it is that I am?
Oh mom, can you see what it is that I am?
I'll be what I'll be, I'll do what I'll do.
Oh mom, can you see I'm just like you?

I hope and I pray that you'll finally see
I've tried to be there for you
And when times are tough, it's you I think of
You're smiling face pulls me through.

Oh mom, can you see what it is that I am?
Oh mom, can you see what it is that I am?
I'll be what I'll be, I'll do what I'll do.
Oh mom, can you see I'm just like you?

Oh mom, can you see what it is that I am?
Oh mom, can you see what it is that I am?
I'll be what I'll be, I'll do what I'll do.
Oh mom, can you see I'm just like you?

TOBY

John has always said he wished he could write something to tell me how much he loves me. He doesn't need to really. All he must do is hold my hand. His first song he shared with Colleen and me was all I needed to hear.

So, during a quiet evening alone I penned this one. **'Oh, my Darling it's You'** was something I wrote feeling his love. I am pretty sure he could write it a little better. He does fantastic writing.

OH, MY DARLING IT'S YOU

Chorus: Oh, my darling it's you who completes my life
My pretty baby all dressed in white.
Oh, my darling it's you who makes me smile
My pretty baby prettiest in sight.

You picked me to be the one
When I asked you out you said OK?
You stayed beside me thick and thin
And I stand beside only you today.

Chorus: Oh, my darling it's you who completes my life
My pretty baby all dressed in white.
Oh, my darling it's you who makes me smile
My pretty baby prettiest in sight.

You smile at me and say I do
I repeat my vows, you start to cry
You promise to love me forever and a day
And I, you too, til the day I die.

Chorus: Oh, my darling it's you who completes my life
My pretty baby all dressed in white.
Oh, my darling it's you who makes me smile
My pretty baby prettiest in sight.

We walk together down the aisle
Forever in love, hand in hand
Throughout our life it's now us
You are my wife and I your husband

Chorus: Oh, my darling it's you who completes my life
My pretty baby all dressed in white.
Oh, my darling it's you who makes me smile
My pretty baby prettiest in sight.

KAL 03/11/14

'Rockin' Baby Love' was a collaboration. John and I have always wanted to write together. Some make sense and some don't. I love this one.

It was about the time John started dropping the country songs and started his love of Blues and return to some of his Rock and Roll days.

ROCKIN' LOVE BABY

George, Garth & Alan helped ease away my blues.
Their songs made me realize I had nothing left to lose.
So, I brushed the dust off my old guitar
Started playing, and then I met her...

Now I'm rockin' to a new beat, no worries or cares.
The louder I play my music, the more love she shares.

C: She's my rockin' love baby and I'm her lovin' blues man.
Can't remember life before her, never want my cloud to land.

I've got me a good woman, and we're rockin' every night.
No more country songs for me, my lady rocks me outa sight.

C: She's my rockin' love baby and I'm her lovin' blues man.
Can't remember life before her, never want my cloud to land.
She's my rockin' love baby and I'm her lovin' blues man.
Can't remember life before her, never want my cloud to land.

KAL & BUB 04/23/09

This is a direct remembrance I think to when John and I went to a movie as friends and ended up finding out we were both floundering in our marriages and personal life.

We were friends and didn't approach being totally in love until we had left Ontario and landed in British Columbia. John was in love first. I was tentative because I didn't have the turmoil, he had in his first marriage. Mine was just done one day. His blew up in his face – truly in his face. His first wife was not a very nice person. Especially to John. She used him and he was afraid to fail so went along with her tantrums. But Christmas 1995 was not a good one for John. He found out that she was running around with another man and had told everyone they were engaged also. John was still fighting for that marriage. My heart was so sad for him.

And over time we found a love so strong that nothing could come between it. A few disagreements and heartaches and we still like to hold hands. I am so proud to be his wife. I don't deserve such a love. John is true blue and full of so much love for his family.

'Rock on, rock hard' we kind of wrote in between life and I'm not sure if we worked on it at all?

ROCK ON, ROCK HARD

Rock on, rock hard, play the music loud.
Play now, play long, beat out the sound.

Don't ever let it fade, keep the fire lit all night.
Can't afford to stop now, play till it's daylight.

Rock on, rock hard, play the music loud.
Play now, play long, beat out the sound.

Tonight, it means too much for us to just give in
Think we may have found, one of the last deadly sins.

Rock on, rock hard, play the music loud.
Play now, play long, beat out the sound.

Everyone up on the dance floor & clap into the air
Having lots of fun tonight & we don't really care

Rock on, rock hard, play the music loud.
Play now, play long, beat out the sound.
Rock on, rock hard, play the music loud.
Play now, play long, beat out the sound.

KAL A BUB 04/17/09

One of my first love songs was **'Secret Dreams, Secret Heart'.** It was about being a teenager and being in love with a boy that was certainly out of your reach.

It is having dreams of getting that boy finally. It is also how much we hide behind our eyes. There have been a few boys that I thought 'if he'd only ask me out, I would be in heaven.' But those are secrets within me. I know many didn't even know I existed.

The truth is that those are crushes and it is a good thing that I was never going down that path. God has plans is something I believe in. I trust I am where I am supposed to be. The path may have been rocky with many paths intersecting it, but God showed me the way. If I veered off course, he brought me back to the path I needed most. Thank you, God, for all your love and for giving me choices in life.

SECRET DREAMS, SECRET HEART

Secret dreams, secret heart
Our love can never start
Deep, dark secrets inside of me
Being together will never be

I saw you yesterday, But you looked the other way.
I don't understand, what's the use? I won't let my love on the loose
I can't have you for mine, I know that's true, so fine.
But I can't deny I love you. So, what else is there I can do.

Secret dreams, secret heart
Our love can never start
Deep, dark secrets inside of me
Being together will never be

You'll not know how I feel, I keep on an even keel.
To confess my love, what's the harm? But, oh just to be in your arms.
I know I'll not confess. To keep it hidden is best.
For if you knew, I'd have no dreams. And my love wouldn't be what it
seems.

Secret dreams, secret heart
Our love can never start
Deep, dark secrets inside of me
Being together will never be

Secret dreams, secret heart
Our love can never start
Deep, dark secrets inside of me
Being together will never be

TOBY

When my sister, Colleen, passed away I was in the middle of a life turbulence of my own. I was fighting for my own stability. I lost that battle and ended up being away from my family for six months. I paid the price and I know God steered me there. I am thankful for the few people that I met and keep in touch with.

My grief brought forward a song dedicated to her. Colleen was a bright light in everyone she met. She just made those she loved feel like they were more than enough. She cheered everyone on. She opened her door to all. Colleen was a fantastic and fierce mom and gramma. They came first. But anyone under her umbrella she would stand up for. She was so talented musically. I know if she had taken the path to be a songstress, she would have rocked it. She could here a song and sing it back to you. She taught herself piano tunes and she became very talented on a guitar.

I can imagine she is up in Heaven getting a jamboree going. I smile when I look up to the skies. My big sister is a beautiful angel now. This is untitled but for her.

She played a new tune as she strummed her guitar
Then looked around and noticed she was not alone
It pleased her to know they'd come to hear her play
She gave them the best they'd ever known

Her voice was strong as her foot tapped along
Everyone knew she gave her all in her songs
They all listened and danced as she gave it her all
She yodelled and she smiled, and she stood tall

When God came calling, she tried her very best
To stay a little longer and keep singing her songs
But time came to pass, and God called her home
We didn't want to let go but he needed her to come along

Her voice was strong as her foot tapped along
Everyone knew she gave her all in her songs
They all listened and danced as she gave it her all
She yodelled and she smiled, and she stood tall

Life continues on and we miss her dearly you know
She sings in God's choir and He's happy too
My sister is an angel and watches over us all
In our hearts she's still here and it will have to do.

Her voice was strong as her foot tapped along
Everyone knew she gave her all in her songs
They all listened and danced as she gave it her all
She yodelled and she smiled, and she stood tall

KAL 17/05/04

'She's the kinda woman that needs a lighter touch'. I'll start with saying this one kicked around for a few years. I had this chorus that kept popping up in my head. And finally, one evening I sat down and finished it.

It is a bit about how I saw life for many couples mixed in with a happy ending. How many people have had the opportunity to meet another person briefly that stayed in their memory? I bet there are many.

So, this song is for those that have a little piece of their heart hidden away thinking about what could have been and then jumping at the chance to rekindle with them.

SHE'S THE KINDA WOMAN THAT NEEDS A LIGHTER TOUCH

I was a wild young man, and my women the same.
Living fast, high on life; a soul no one could tame.
Bar room brawls after midnight, spilt into the streets.
Heated arguments with each night's date.

It took a long time for me to turn into a man.
I was 35 before I knew I might've missed my chance.
I remember her in my dreams; quiet, but she set me on fire.
And I walked away from her, knowing she was my desire.

I'd met her a long time ago
-didn't get to know her much.
Cuz she's the kinda woman
That needs a lighter touch.

I was ready to settle down, didn't know if she was on her own.
I had only known her briefly, yet I reach for the phone.
Her voice sounds like an angel I don't know what to say
I have to take this gently; I don't want to scare her away.

I'd met her a long time ago
-didn't get to know her much.
Cuz she's the kinda woman
That needs a lighter touch.

Cuz she's the kinda woman
That needs a lighter touch.

KAL 03/11/24

I will admit I was in love with many boys as a teenager. If I was asked out, I would dream how our lives would be together. I gave each the chance to be the 'one'. And for the most part I wasn't their 'one'. But that is perfectly okay. It gave my imagination a great workout. There were not many that didn't get the consideration.

It was easy to see myself married with children with those that made my heart go pitter-patter. I almost thought I was strange thinking and having these dreams. I have talked to a lot of people, and they admitted to also having love dreams too. Made me feel a lot better.

So, **'Since Our Love Is Through'** was for all those dreams. My mom thought I should write soap operas when I would tell her some of my dreams.

SINCE OUR LOVE IS THROUGH

I Don't Know What To Think
Since You Did What You Did
And I Don't Know What To Feel
Since You Said What You Said
And How Am I Supposed To Care
When I Know That You're Not There?
I Don't Know What To Do
Since Our Love Is Through

I Only Know How To Love You
It's All I've Done For All My Life
You Must Realize What You Have Done
You Can't Love Her And Have Me As Your Wife
And What Am I Supposed To Do
When I Know That You're Untrue?
Even Though I Still Love You
I Know Our Love Is Through

You Must Have Stopped Loving Me
When And How I Don't Know
You'll Have To Make Up Your Own Mind
Just How Much Farther You'll Go
And When You Do, Please Tell Me
Are You Mine Or Am I Free?
I Just Don't Know What To Do
Since Our Love Is Through.

TOBY

This is one of my favourite songs. It is for my mom and my sister, Colleen, and I sang it for Mother's Day one year at church. I added the last four lines after my mom passed away.

Every time I sing it I get a tear in my eye. I trust that my mom has heard it many times when she pops in to check on me from time to time. I harmonize in my van to this song a lot. My grandsons have asked me to sing it to them Jayson use to say, 'Gramma please sing mama's knee to me'.

'Sitting at My Mama's Knee' is for my mom, and I am so appreciative that she got to hear it at church and when I sent her a tape with it on. She loved it.

SITTING AT MY MAMA'S KNEE

Times are changing fast; I just can't keep up.
I'm having trouble doing what is right.
Mama, she did warn me it would be hard
Life is an uphill fight.
I really could use some memories
Just to go back to the way it use to be.
I remember things that I use to hear.
Sitting at my Mama's knee

Like when little sis, she made such a fuss
Just because our brother rode her bike too fast
Or when my best friend said she didn't like me.
Mama said it wouldn't last.
Many broken hearts were mended by my mom
As I spilled my woes, she'd sit so patiently
These were the times you'd find me
Sitting at my Mama's knee.

I learned about love, and I learned about trust
And about God, who loves us from above
It's things like these that mean so much to me
Just like my Mama's love
Life was much more fun when I was young
I long for the days when Mama sang to me
I wish I could go back and curl up on the floor
And sit at my Mama's knee.

I really could use some memories
Just to go back to the way it use to be
I remember things that I use to hear.
Sitting at my Mama's knee.
Now that she is gone; I really need her more
Look at me standing staring at the door.
I wish God would bring my Mama back to me
So, I could sit at my Mama's knee.

TOBY

'Spinning Like a Top' was a feeling inside. I was alone for my birthday. Separated from all my loved one. I was feeling sorry for myself to be honest.

I had lived through something I never thought I would have to. I paid my dues and wanted to do nothing more than come home to my family. I guess that was a little selfish. I keep coming back to that word lately.

Why after so much giving would someone that I love unconditionally to say I was selfish – that I always have been. I think if I was selfish, I would never have married the men I did or never married at all. If I were selfish, I would have found a rich man and never had children. That is what I think.

But for my own blood to stab that into my back was horrible. How do you get back from that? I still love my son, but I fear he may never know how to apologize for the heartless words he has said.

SPINNING LIKE A TOP

Spinning like a top, my life continues on.
I'm up, I'm down. I hear an endless sound.
Spinning like a top, my life continues on.
I'm up, I'm down. I hear an endless sound.
Spinning like a top, my life continues on.
I'm up, I'm down. I hear an endless sound.

Spinning like a top, my life continues on.
I'm up, I'm down. I hear an endless sound.

NO, I'm not going to take it anymore
And I don't care if I slam the front door
I'm going to kick up my heels & get out of town
And I don't care if he does or doesn't make a sound.

NO, I'm not going to take it anymore
And I don't care if I slam the front door
I'm going to kick up my heels & get out of town
And I don't care if he does or doesn't make a sound.

NO, I'm not going to take it anymore
And I don't care if I slam the front door
I'm going to kick up my heels & get out of town
And I don't care if he does or doesn't make a sound.
NO, I'm not going to take it anymore
And I don't care if I slam the front door
I'm going to kick up my heels & get out of town
And I don't care if he does or doesn't make a sound.

Finding it so hard to balance myself today.
Yesterday was better; tomorrow come what may.
Wanting to do more with my time at hand
Searching around me, where will I land?
Seeing it all through, up to the very end.
Believing I'm okay until the angels are sent.

TOBY 17/09/23

'Staying Right Here'. John started this song at some point, and I came across the unfinished song. I hope he likes how I changed it up a little.

Sometimes I will find half finished songs of my own or of John's and decide to see where it will take me.

I can't walk away from these songs. They deserve to be finished. We all deserve to have our songs finished. Whether it is about life or just a bunch of words on a scrap piece of paper.

STAYING RIGHT HERE

Around the corner, just out of sight
Is where I stay throughout the night

You are so out of my reach, can't seem to get your eye
I might as well go home, lay down and cry

Staying right here, just out of sight
Keeping my attraction lost in the bright lights

You are so out of my reach, can't seem to get your eye
I might as well go home, lay down and cry

You look across the room, just beyond me
It's never me, but someone else you see.

You are so out of my reach, can't seem to get your eye
I might as well go home, lay down and cry

You are so out of my reach, can't seem to get your eye
I might as well go home, lay down and cry

Staying right here, just out of sight
Your eyes meet mine and this is the night
Staying right here, just out of sight
You are in my arms and feels so right!

KAL & BUB 03/23/09

'Twitterpation' Now here is a fun one. Shawn Winter and I envisioned the band, and we had a lot of fun getting together and being creative. We were sitting around working on a few songs that Shawn liked and this popped in my head. I wrote it down and gave it to Shawn to put music to. Winter Pressey Band never sang in front of some family. We never had the chance since I was moving to BC and taking the music collaborator I lined up for Shawn. Nevertheless, we did have a few great sessions.

There is no reference to the Disney movie other than that word. And for us it was a reference to being all crazy in love with someone. *'Twitterpation'* was how we felt.

TWITTERPATION

My body is a-shaking, and I heat up in the night.
My hands are a-twitching, and my eyes don't focus right.
The doc says I could get a second opinion
Cause he says what I've got is TWITTERPATION
My heart plays a tune and drums a loud beat.
My head feels so light my temperature's a-heat
The doc says I'll just have to give in
Cause no one can fight it – TWITTERPATION
Now don't be afraid cause I wear a silly grin.
Having what I have isn't a major sin
Many folks have it – you may just be one
Doc says we all get it – TWITTERPATION
My lips are a-trembling, and they crave a certain kiss
My arms reach out for someone who has this
I can see in your eye's anticipation
The doc says you too have TWITTERPATION

TOBY 95/09/25

I'd love to say this was about John because he is exactly the man I am supposed to be with. Steve was my 'fall into' love. I love him still but not infatuated with him anymore. Steve was a cushion to make my heart realize that my efforts into my marriage had ceased. He made me look at Jay and decide if what we had would be enough for life. As much as it hurt me, I saw the end.

'The Way of Life for Me' was my acceptance that maybe I was in love with someone else. Maybe it was Steve or maybe not. There was that little bit of uncertainty that nibbled away in my brain. Steve was willing to be there for me. He convinced me I needed to release myself and start to live again. It didn't happen suddenly as we wrote for almost a year before we decided maybe there was still something there.

The last thing I wanted to do was hurt Jay, but no one realized Jay left our marriage first. He shut down. He stopped trying. I don't blame him for that. I was always busy. We didn't get a lot of time together alone. My focus for the last five years of my marriage was my kids. Keeping them happy and in sports or groups. Nothing pleased me more than watching them play baseball. I was so proud when they excelled, and I did whatever I could to make sure they stayed busy also.

Steve said he would be there for my kids too, but I had a hard time thinking that would happen. He had never had his own children and I am sure did not realize himself how much time and effort there is. At the last moment it wasn't in the card for Steve and me to be together. I know in my heart I made a right decision there.

THE WAY OF LIFE FOR ME

Somewhere in the night,
I'm sure I heard him say,
I need you by my side
Please come to me today
But as much as I wanted then
I could not return his plea,
Because I gave my love away
And that was the way of life for me.

I did not ask him to wait
Until I was set free
But I'm sure that he would have
Because I knew he loved me.
Instead, I thought of him alone
And cried to myself at night.
And when I needed his love
I'd just hug my pillow tight

Somehow, I saw that through
And prayed to God above
That sometimes I could be his
And return all that special love
So, each night I thought of him
And gazed out at the moon
I hoped he heard my call
That I'd be with him soon

Somewhere in the night
I know I heard him say
I'll always love you so
And I'm glad you're here today
God was listening to my prayers
And now I can return his plea
For now, I give him all my love
He's now the way of life for me.

TOBY 95/10/01

My stint in 'Camp Cupcake' had me getting lonely and feeling so displaced from my family. No regrets for protecting others but still was something that gave me a lot of time to reflect.

'Waiting' was one night feeling alone and trying to let my family know I was okay, but I was lonely. I asked for no visitors. The trip would be over 10 hours one way for anyone. I am not a person that wants to put others out.

Although I can't stop remembering my son saying I was selfish. I am sure I can be at times like just about everyone on the planet. I do not agree that I think only of myself. I would never have landed at 'Camp Cupcake' otherwise. I never fought for my right to tell the truth that would have uprooted many people and their families. I said nothing and accepted the blame myself. Selfish of me, I guess. Still, I was waiting for the time to be back with my family including the son that has disowned me because I have different opinions and political views. Hmmm......selfish of me or is that selfish of himself. I have many family members and friends that see things different than me and we love each other without having to discuss all that. I pray one day to see his family again. I miss hugging my three granddaughters. They mean so much to me, but maybe I shouldn't as I must be thinking of myself and the anguish of not seeing them.

WAITING

Waiting, waiting, waiting
Wanting, wanting, wanting
Feeling, feeling, feeling
Needing, needing, needing

I wait to hear from anyone and you
I want to feel close again to you
I feel so sad not being there
I need to know what to do

Waiting, waiting, waiting
Wanting, wanting, wanting
Feeling, feeling, feeling
Needing, needing, needing

You wait to hear from me
You want to be a part of me
You feel sad that I am here
You need for me to be free.

Waiting, waiting, waiting
Wanting, wanting, wanting
Feeling, feeling, feeling
Needing, needing, needing

We wait for each other now
We want to renew our love
We feel that there has to be more
We need to pray to God above

Waiting, waiting, waiting
Wanting, wanting, wanting
Feeling, feeling, feeling
Needing, needing, needing

KAL 17/04/26

'We are Girl Guides'. I wrote during my leadership of Girl Guides in Straffordville, Ontario. I was hoping to teach it to the girls and have a little fun. I wasn't brave enough and the district didn't want the girls to learn it. They wanted approval from Regional and National and World. So here it is. It isn't anything bold. It was just something to have fun with.

WE ARE GIRL GUIDES

We Are Girl Guides........We Are Girl Guides
We Are Girl Guides........We Are Girl Guides

We Are Girl Guides
Look At Us Now
We've Grown To Be
So True And Proud
We Took All Our Hopes
And Tossed Them In The Air
And We Found Out
There's A World That Cares

We Are Girl Guides........We Are Girl Guides
We Are Girl Guides........We Are Girl Guides

As Trusted As Can Be
We're Loyal And Strong
We're Helpful To You
Never Let A Friend Do Wrong
We Try To Be Kind
To Everyone We Meet
And We Obey Orders
We're Hard To Beat

We Are Girl Guides........We Are Girl Guides
We Are Girl Guides........We Are Girl Guides

We'll Smile The Day Through
And Sing Out Our Hearts
We Love This Earth
So, To Conserve Is Our Part
With Pure Thought, Word
And Deeds, We Never Hide
That We Are Glad
To Be Part Of Girl Guides

We Are Girl Guides........We Are Girl Guides
We Are Girl Guides........We Are Girl Guides

We Are Girl Guides........We Are Girl Guides We Are Girl
Guides........We Are Girl Guides

TOBY

'We all need a romantic song' was for John and John alone. I wanted to let him know how much I love him and how he was such a deciding factor in my life. The love he gave me healed many wounds.

I was also thinking of calling it **'You Came Into My Life'.** There is always a change of title when writing a song. Sometimes the title just doesn't fit right. I have changed a few over the years. So maybe at some point this one will be changed also.

John is the love of my life. The final chapter to who I am. He helped me through a few of the most difficult times of my life. I thank God for him every day. All people need to have a spouse just like him. He's not perfect, but he's perfect for me.

WE ALL NEED A ROMANTIC SONG

We all need a romantic song
To pull our hearts along
We all need a somebody too
To do all we need to do.

You came into my life
Did something to my thoughts
You came into my life
Made me more out of life want
You came into my life
And turned my heart upside down
You came into my life
Made a smile from a frown

We all need a romantic song
To pull our hearts along
We all need a somebody too
To do all we need to do.

You came into my life
Caused a stir within my heart
You came into my life
Blew all my plans far apart
You came into my life
Knowing the troubles inside
You came into my life
Told me I no longer had to hide

We all need a romantic song
To pull our hearts along
We all need a somebody too
To do all we need to do.

We all need a romantic song
To pull our hearts along
We all need a somebody too
To do all we need to do.

TOBY 96/05/12

'We Didn't Talk' is an ode to Jay more or less. It is about how our love ended and me getting the nerve to be brave and start again. I love the song and the momentum to leaving. It does say how I felt the day I drove away.

I was unsure of everything. I know Jay thought I would get out to British Columbia and come back home. I thought that may happen also. I waited for the school year to end and longing to find out when the kids could come to see the area. Didn't happen but I kept my chin up that someday they would.

Jay showed his manipulative side, and the kids were afraid to leave him. I was not happy when my youngest son said his dad would be too sad and just die if any on them moved to be with me. I couldn't bring myself to fight for them to come, just hope they would make that decision on their own.

WE DIDN'T TALK

We didn't talk, we didn't fight
Although I stayed up for him every night
He'd come through the door, he'd head for the shower
I had become his little wallflower.

If ever I was right, I was then wrong
Nothing mattered to him all along
He'd go for a jog, he'd just run away
Never listened to what I had to say.
I'm gonna dress up in a pair of new shoes
Hey buddy, I've got nothing here to lose
He should have paid more attention to me
Because now I'm gonna find a new me.

The time came to leave, he didn't stop me
After all these years he'd now set me free
This flower had bloomed, it was too late
Hanging around was my biggest mistake.

We didn't talk, we didn't fight
And now he can watch me drive out of sight......

TOBY 13/06/15

One of my earlier writings from just before I was marrying Jay. I had worries but I also knew I loved him, and my rose-colored glasses told me I was up for the challenge. I kept this one tucked away in my notepad for quite a while. I should have sung it for Jay at least once. He might have realized I was willing to fight for him. **'What is it about this day'** was for Jay.

Someone had to fight for him. I had nightmares that if I didn't stay, he would end up under a taxi outside a bar in St. Thomas like his uncle had. I wish he could have seen his own potential like I did. He could have gotten his GED. He could have applied himself to a career. Any career he wanted. His expectations were much lower of himself though. It was a challenge for sure and I was happy that I had gotten him to where he was working. I got tired and that is on me.

I thought love could make everything better and we could weather anything we came up against. We did a few challenges then life got too busy for both of us.

WHAT IS IT ABOUT THIS DAY?

What is it about this day
That makes me want to cry?
What is it about our life
That brings a tear to my eye?
I've thought a lot lately
About how i feel for you
Are we giving our all, our very all
The best that we can do.

We've been together quite awhile
You and I
Has our love dwindled down
Or is it still at a high?
It just seems to me
That we often forget
To say our love out loudly,
Like when we first met

So, with this day
Being our happiest,
I promise you, always,
That I love you best.
So, when it comes the very time
To vow our love so true,
Just remember I'm the one
Who'll say, "I love you."

What is it about this day
That makes me want to cry?
What is it about our life
That brings a tear to my eye?
What is it about this day
That makes me want to cry?
What is it about this day
That brings a tear to my eye?

TOBY

I wrote **'What's it going to take'** again for Jay. After I left and Jay knew I wanted the kids to come out he tried to convince me I should come home. His plea wasn't for the kids. It was only for himself. I still wasn't sure if my friendship with John was going to go anywhere yet. But I knew enough that I couldn't go backwards. I had to do this and make life right again.

WHAT'S IT GOING TO TAKE

What's it going to take, to convince you we are through
What's it going to take, to make you realize I don't love you.

I've tried many ways to talk about this to you
I've tried many times but what am I to do.
You don't listen to me when I start to talk
You don't care to hear me, it's out the door you walk

What's it going to take, to convince you we are through
What's it going to take, to make you realize I don't love you.

We can't keep all this up when there's nothing left for us.
We can't keep denying this, it's not you but him I love so much
Every time I start to leave, you pretend there's more to our love.
Every time I think I can go, you say our love is more than enough

What's it going to take, to convince you we are through
What's it going to take, to make you realize I don't love you.

What's it going to take, to convince you we are through
What's it going to take, to make you realize I don't love you.

TOBY 96/04/07

I remember writing this next one crying in my room upstairs at the farm. A tender teenager and having your real first love leave. Yes, it was Steve. He left a few times in our 'on and off again' relationship. He bruised my heart, and I was ecstatic each time he returned. Never questioned him why. I was just happy to be with him again. I know my family all thought I would marry Steve I mean my full name is Kimberley and if I married him, I could be Kim Byerlay. It worked.

So, the last time he was the one to walk away I wrote this one promising myself it would never happen again. (It did a couple more time, but I walked away). **'Whatcha going to do'** is about young love and wishing it could be the last love. Most people I know have had that one that was always showing back up.

WHATCHA GOIN' TO DO NOW?

Whatcha goin' to do now that I'm gone?
Who you goin' to depend on?
Whatcha goin' to do now that I'm away?
Who's goin' to brighten up your day?

I loved you with all my heart,
But how can I now that we're apart?
I loved you as much as I could
Who's goin' to love you like they should?

Whatcha goin' to do now that I'm gone?
Who you goin' to depend on?
Whatcha goin' to do now that I'm away?
Who's goin' to brighten up your day?

It was your idea to let me go
Even though it hurt me so.
I loved you, it was plain to see
And I thought you loved me.

Whatcha goin' to do now that I'm gone?
Who you goin' to depend on?
Whatcha goin' to do now that I'm away?
Who's goin' to brighten up your day?

Who's goin' to be with you tonight?
Who's goin' to love you with all their might?
Who's goin' to make you feel so good?
Just the way a man should?

Whatcha goin' to do now that I'm gone?
Who you goin' to depend on?
Whatcha goin' to do now that I'm away?
Who's goin' to brighten up your day?

Whatcha goin' to do now that I'm gone?
Who you goin' to depend on?
Whatcha goin' to do now that I'm away?
Who's goin' to brighten up your day?

Whatcha goin' to do now that I'm gone?
Whatcha goin' to do now that I'm gone?
Whatcha goin' to do now that I'm gone?

TOBY

I was floundering in the first few months of 1996. There I was married, yet we were not happy. I had Steve trying to convince me to rip off the Band-Aid and do something for myself and for him. Then bam there was John befriending me and listening to both sides of my life. At that moment in time, I would have stayed with Jay if he had asked me to and changed his outlook on life also. If Steve had showed up at the front door and said, 'baby I'm here to whisk you away and help you heal', I would have blindly followed him. And there was John again. I wasn't sure of my feelings for him, but he was being a great listener and friend.

'When You are So Far Away' could be for Steve as he was far away. It may have been for Jay who was not present in the marriage right then. Maybe it was for John who was a long-haul trucker. That time in my life is a blur. I think that was a good thing as I was growing sadder and thinner as each day passed.

And just for the record to everyone it was not for my baseball friend Bob. He was a great shoulder to lean on and help me navigate my life when my dad became ill with his brain tumours. Bob was just 'Bob' – he helped everyone.

WHEN YOU'RE SO FAR AWAY

I know that lately I've been amiss
I didn't say I loved you or your lips did I kiss.
I find I want you more and more each passing day
But how can I really love you when you're so far away

Tell my why did we do it –
I mean go separate ways,
Tell me why we didn't
I love you more say.
Maybe tomorrow
Will show us what to do
Cause I'm willing to forgive
Forget and say I need you

I know that lately I've been amiss
I didn't say I loved you or your lips did I kiss.
I find I want you more and more each passing day
But how can I really love you when you're so far away

Why didn't we see it
Before our love was gone?
Why didn't we notice
We were drifting all along?
Could it be we weren't meant to be
Together for all of our lives?
Are we looking honestly
At us or is it all lies?

I know that lately I've been amiss
I didn't say I loved you or your lips did I kiss.
I find I want you more and more each passing day
But how can I really love you when you're so far away

TOBY 96/02/23

I had a brief lonesome time in 2017. My own problem. Being away from John was so hard. I couldn't touch him or hug him. At best I would talk to him once a week. I felt so cut-off from life and insecurities mounted as I would try and fall asleep at night. I counted the days. I pray to God frequently. I didn't discuss my thoughts much with many. Maybe with Kristy as she also had some insecurities. We meshed and keep in touch. She was a breath of fresh air as she was a normal person at 'Camp Cupcake;'

'Who Am I?' came to light from my own insecurities. I had to release the song from within or I would have gone crazy.

WHO AM I?

Chorus: Who am I without you?
What am I without you?
How will I live without you?
Where will I go without you?

I need you to stay in my life
Let me continue to be your loving wife
I need you to understand me
You are my love, why can't you see?

Chorus: Who am I without you?
What am I without you?
How will I live without you?
Where will I go without you?

You were always mine from the start
Why would we ever want to part?
You are the only one I've ever loved
Why are you going, I've asked God above?

Chorus: Who am I without you?
What am I without you?
How will I live without you?
Where will I go without you?

We have been one for such a long time
Without you around I have nothing that's mine
We should remember our vows so true
You need me as I'll always need you

Chorus: Who am I without you?
What am I without you?
How will I live without you?
Where will I go without you?
Chorus: Who am I without you?   (Start fading)
What am I without you?
How will I live without you?
Where will I go without you?

KAL 17/04/23

Why Can't You See?' combines a few boyfriends I had as a teenager. There was Steve who came and went as you know. There was Bailey who seemed to be who I was frequently matched up with whenever someone needed a date for him so they could go as a double date. There was Romi who called up every so often to go out. Apparently Romi was heart broken when I was getting married. I didn't know that until the week before I was married, and he told me the girl he was in love with was getting married and not to him. I can't forget Jeff who I'm sure I should have paid more attention to as he would have been true if I gave him my heart. I had a couple flings with Barry who wasn't interested in a long-term relationship. There were others but I am not ashamed to say were mostly just one-night hook ups here and there.

WHY CAN'T YOU SEE?

Ah-ah-ah, Why can't you see?
Ah-ah-ah, You mean everything to me!
Ah-ah-ah, I'll never leave you.
Ah-ah-ah, I love only you.

Outside it's cold and lonely
Inside, there's always me.
Couldn't you try to believe
Not all women try to deceive.

Ah-ah-ah, Why can't you see?
Ah-ah-ah, You mean everything to me!
Ah-ah-ah, I'll never leave you.
Ah-ah-ah, I love only you.

Maybe sometime you'll trust me
And then my love you'll see.
Try to look deep in my eyes
See past all other's lies.

Ah-ah-ah, Why can't you see?
Ah-ah-ah, You mean everything to me!
Ah-ah-ah, I'll never leave you.
Ah-ah-ah, I love only you.

I'll wait forever for you
To decide what you want to do
Whenever you can love me
You'll know where I'll always be

Ah-ah-ah, Why can't you see?
Ah-ah-ah, You mean everything to me!
Ah-ah-ah, I'll never leave you.
Ah-ah-ah, I love only you.

Ah-ah-ah, Why can't you see?
Ah-ah-ah, You mean everything to me!
Ah-ah-ah, I'll never leave you.
Ah-ah-ah, I love only you.

TOBY

When I started writing to Steve in 1995 it was as friends. We tap-danced around our love life. I told him all about being married and my children and what they had done. We wrote about people we used to know and if we had seen them lately. He helped me with my grief of my dad's passing, and I was helping him with his parent's passing also.

I don't think either of us were expecting the old feelings to come back until it was too late. All it took was one simple question. Are you happy? I told him I loved my children. I even loved Jay. Again, he asked, 'Are you happy though?'
It was then I realized that I wasn't. I started evaluating my life.

He called me one night and it was like we were teenagers again. It was a long conversation each time. And the letters came two to three times a week back and forth. I never hid them from Jay. He never asked me either. If he had I don't know where I would be today. Would I still be in Ontario and celebrating over forty years married? Would it just delay the end?

Then Steve said he was coming down to see me. I didn't tell him not to. I wanted to see if it was real. It was real. We talked for three hours. It was exhilarating to have someone who listened and talked to me. After he went back home, he wrote me and told me when I was ready, he would be waiting for me. He said to tell Jay if he didn't want to be my husband then he would be glad to make me his wife. I never got to that part with Jay. Inside I was hoping Jay would tell me he was coming too. **'Why Didn't you Tell me?'** was what I wrote about. It takes a little about Jay and a lot about Steve into account.

WHY DIDN'T YOU TELL ME?

Why didn't you tell me
What was on your mind?
Why didn't you tell me
Things would work our fine?

I didn't realize then
How much I'd miss you
I didn't realize this
Till we were through
We could have made a go
Right from the start
We could have saved
Ourselves broken hearts.

Why didn't you tell me
What was on your mind?
Why didn't you tell me
Things would work our fine?

You must have felt the same
All those years ago
You must have felt
How much I loved you so
Should've stayed together
Not drifted apart
Should've known our love
Was strong right from the start.

Why didn't you tell me
What was on your mind?
Why didn't you tell me
Things would work our fine?

You made me smile
You're back in my life
You fixed my heart
Now we're husband and wife
I know we've waited
For a long, long, time.
You know you should've
Told me things would work our fine.

Why didn't you tell me
What was on your mind?
Why didn't you tell me
Things would work our fine?

TOBY 10//01

'Why don't you Love me?' was after I had met John. I think it was my first song with him in my mind even though we weren't thinking much about that then. We were comforting each other. John is such a great guy. I will say I had to teach him to stop saying 'I'm sorry' all the time.

When we would talk about our children and our lives, I imagined him kissing me, hugging me, holding me, and loving me. But I was still in love with my husband and loved Steve. It was a whirlwind time for my brain. I was confused. I was lost. I was……. almost suicidal. There I said it. I would never have done that. John helped me over a lot of ruts and potholes.

WHY DON'T YOU LOVE ME?

Why Don't You Love Me? Why Don't You Love Me?
Why Don't You Kiss Me? Why Don't You Kiss Me?
Why Don't You Hug Me? Why Don't You Hug Me?
Why Don't You Love Me? Why Don't You Love Me?

I never knew that I'd love
Someone like you so strong.
I never thought I'd feel this
It's been gone away so long.
Now that I feel this love
I don't want to give it up.
Why Don't You Love Me? Why Don't You Love Me?
Why Don't You Kiss Me? Why Don't You Kiss Me?
Why Don't You Hug Me? Why Don't You Hug Me?
Why Don't You Love Me? Why Don't You Love Me?

I never thought you'd love me
Half as much as I love you
I need to feel my body
Close up to only you
So, baby come and see me
Show me just how much you love me
Why Don't You Love Me? Why Don't You Love Me?
Why Don't You Kiss Me? Why Don't You Kiss Me?
Why Don't You Hug Me? Why Don't You Hug Me?
Why Don't You Love Me? Why Don't You Love Me?

I'm going to tell you now
I need to see you
I'm going to tell you how
How much I want you
And baby you can find out
My love is deep, I want to shout.....
Why Don't You Love Me? Why Don't You Love Me?
Why Don't You Kiss Me? Why Don't You Kiss Me?
Why Don't You Hug Me? Why Don't You Hug Me?
Why Don't You Love Me? Why Don't You Love Me?

REPEAT   96/03/15

'Wondering if you know' was never a song about me. It just came to me, and I couldn't get it out of my head. I don't have a melody for it yet, but the lyrics were there.

Often, I have weird ideas, words, thoughts, poems, songs pop into my head. It could be from someone close to me. It could be just a feeling I picked up from my dreams. Who knows as they just come up?

WONDERING IF YOU KNOW

…. Keep checking my phone to make sure it's on.

Haven't heard from you for way, way too long.

Wondering if you know how much I've missed you.

Thinking that maybe it was too good to be true.

…. Keep checking my phone to make sure it's on.

Haven't heard from you for way, way too long.

Thought our love was going to make it thru.

Maybe I should have said more "I love you's"

…. Keep checking my phone to make sure it's on.

Haven't heard from you for way, way too long.

Guess our love wasn't meant to be or very true.

Time to look elsewhere, that's what I should do.

…. Turning off my phone, don't care if you call.

Won't talk to you again, I don't care at all.

(Phone rings………. hello, oh so glad you called….
Yes, I love you baby……)

TOBY 04/17/09

John gets credit for quite a few of my songs as they are about him. He hasn't heard them all. Well, he is hearing impaired. He hasn't had the opportunity to even read them. I have a hard time sharing my works. Writing this book for my songs and one for my poetry has been my bucket list. I pray I get them published.

I hope John can take the time to read them as he is in a lot. **'Yesterday, Today & Tomorrow'** is with John in my mind and heart. I spun it into a song that John might have sung. The feelings are in reverse from me to him.

YESTERDAY, TODAY & TOMORROW

It's a long stretch of road we're on
But your love keeps us together
We've been through rougher years
Yet, overcome all our deep fears
You've been there for me, now I for you
There isn't anything I wouldn't do for you

Chorus: Yesterday, we were young and carefree
Today, it's a challenge for you and me
Tomorrow, we'll face together, my love
Bring what may, but please God above
Take care of my darling sweet lady
She's my one love, my only baby.

Yesterday was full of struggle and smiles
Today is spent together thinking of the many miles
Tomorrow will surely come and I need you
To be my special lady, pull me through
I'll hold on tight to you lying in my arms
Keep you away from heartache and harm.

Chorus: Yesterday, we were young and carefree
Today, it's a challenge for you and me
Tomorrow, we'll face together, my love
Bring what may, but please God above
Take care of my darling sweet lady
She's my one love, my only baby.

Chorus: Yesterday, we were young and carefree
Today, it's a challenge for you and me
Tomorrow, we'll face together, my love
Bring what may, but please God above
Take care of my darling sweet lady
She's my one love, my only baby.

TOBY 03/12/05

'You won't make a move on me' was for John. It was me telling him we were friends and that we won't ever be free. It was a goodbye song as Steve had said he would take me to British Columbia. I had talked to my former boss who was in Cranbrook, and he had a job for me. As John and I were just friends and even though there was something there we wouldn't explore further.

So many changes in such a short time. It boggles the mind.

YOU WON'T MAKE A MOVE ON ME

You won't make a move on me, And I won't make a move either.
So, let's just say that our love will never be Because we're afraid to love
each other.

I noticed that you were looking my way
But as soon as I did, I turned away
Because every time our eyes do meet
I don't know bout you, but my legs go weak
And try as I might, I can't deny
For some odd reason I want to cry.

You won't make a move on me, And I won't make a move either.
So, let's just say that our love will never be Because we're afraid to love
each other.

I hope I'm safe from my own thoughts
Even if staying away hurts a lot.
You won't cross over that line
Because for us love is at the wrong time
But it gets harder for me each day
To deny our love and push those thoughts away.

You won't make a move on me, And I won't make a move either.
So, let's just say that our love will never be Because we're afraid to love
each other.

I know it's the wrong time for you and me
Because both you and I are not free.
It's better if we not see each other again
Cause even though I'm afraid, it's driving me insane.
Maybe some day things won't be the same
And if they aren't, I'll be happy to change.

You won't make a move on me, And I won't make a move either.
So, let's just say that our love will never be Because we're afraid to love
each other.

TOBY 96/01/10

And to the final song alphabetically, **'You'll never see'.** This was a long, lonely night waiting up for my husband, Jay to come home from work. He was done at 1am and it was a fifteen-minute walk home. So, at 4am I knew he was out drinking. I cried a little, I got mad a little, I had a hot bath, I wrote a song.

As he strolled in around 6am drunk, I closed the bedroom door and went to bed. He knew he had done wrong. We didn't have a big fight over it. More like he was sadly sorry, and I was disgustedly disappointed.

I can't say how many times I felt this way when we were first married. It took a few years for us to click into marriage together. We made it work. We knew we wanted kids so that was our focus. And as each baby came our lives seemed to be melded more and more together. I loved having the kids around and Jay was a great dad.

YOU'LL NEVER SEE

Well, I did it again, my eyes are red and sore.
But you'll never see, through to my core.

I'll cover everything up, my feelings will never show,
You'll think I'm happy, my sadness you'll never know.

Cause you'll never see
Just how lonely I am,
And you'll never know
Why else you're just a man
You'll never see
Just how lonely I am
And you'll never know
Why else you're just a man

You'll never see, just how lonely I am.
You'll never know, I'll be silent as a lamb.

Things may seem the same, between you and me
But underneath it all, I really won't be me.

Cause you'll never see
Just how lonely I am,
And you'll never know
Why else you're just a man
You'll never see
Just how lonely I am
And you'll never know
Why else you're just a man

TOBY

I love to write poetry and songs. I love to sing and talk. I love all my children Jaymee, Kayla, Joshua, and Krychelle. I love John. I love my stepchildren Bill, Becky, and Sean. I loved Jay. I loved Steve.

I am a gramma to a host of beautiful, smart grandchildren. Blood and by choice. Josh, Katie, Lukas, Everley, Eden, Lennon, Jayson, Leland, Jaylynn, Brooklyn, Mekhi, Mya, Brittney, Braden, Asher, Keaunna, James, Jesse, Frank, Sophie. I am not sure there will be any more after Brooklyn our youngest grandchild. I love each of them with all my heart, even those not close enough to hug or see.

As I write this, I have a tune in my head. I have so many more songs and poems to get onto paper. My bucket may have to grow a little more.

I haven't shared with many that I may have to cut all that short as well as life gets in the way, death can also do the same. If it does, I am ready, and the words will remain with me for eternity.

My wish to everyone is to know who you are, be who you are, love who you can, live life the best, and never settle for less.

Take chances in love and life. Be willing to learn and pass on your knowledge. Do not be afraid to say what you are thinking and prepared to back up what you said.

If you are not sure what you should do, ask questions. Life is too short to not take a few chances. Own up to your mistakes. Never, ever throw someone under a bus – even if they deserve it. It will not help, and it will not make you feel better. To those I protected you are welcome. To those who judged me – you know not the whole story. To those who came and went in my life – it is all for a reason. To those who stood up for me – I salute you!

This is not the end, only the beginning. Whether a person had died or is living there is more. Memories keep spirits alive. When you have been forgotten there should still be some lingering.

I lived, I loved, I laughed, I cried. I was here and I was there. I will remain after I am gone. I will touch my loved ones when they need me regardless. Look for me in the sky, in a flower, in a gentle breeze and sometimes in a feather or a butterfly. I am always there just when you will need me. Have faith you are not alone. When the clock hits 1:23 I'll be with one of my loved ones, checking in.

The shadow has lived a long time in my memory along with all the people and places I have been. To understand the shadow, you need to read my poetry book 'Hell's Shadow in Heaven'. It explains why I have had a shadow in my life.

If you allow music into your life, it can dim any shadow. Songs and poems both are constructive tools to coping. Each time I read one of my songs or poems I can feel a little safer, a little at ease, a little more like the woman I thought I could be.

Go forth and be your best person you can be. Live a little and let your inner child loose occasionally. Reach out to someone that has made a difference in your life and stay out of the shadows. Find something that allows you to push the shadows in your life to the background. It will always be part of you, but it doesn't have to control who you are anymore.

Love, KAL

ABOUT THE AUTHOR

Kim Burgess took the pen name of TOBY in 1974 and changed it to KAL in 1996. Under these pen names she has created many poems, musical compositions, and verses. Kim is the youngest of seven children and raised in Southwestern Ontario. As she has always said, she was one of the second Corinthians living in the garden of Eden which is just down the road from the land of Goshen. She will also tell you she had to leave Eden to find Heaven which is Cranbrook BC.

Family members, events and just inspirations were her start in writing. She also admired her paternal grandpa, Leslie Winfred Pressey, as he would sit at his table and hum his own songs over and over with verses he had written. Kim feels that if at least one person is made to feel a little lighter and happier, then she has achieved her purpose.

To Tree – Thanks for your input and insights. To Sherry – Thanks buddy you were the best. To John – I thank God every day for you in my life. To my children and grandchildren – I am because you are.

We all have bumps in the road, but with the love and support of family and friends we can overcome all hardships. Thank you for being my people and my circus!

May your future be bright, alive, and successful.

Kim Burgess//KAL/TOBY